REFUGEE RESETTLEMENT AND THE HIJRA TO AMERICA

By Ann Corcoran

CIVILIZATION JIHAD READER SERIES

Refugee Resettlement and the Hijra to America
is published in the United States by the Center for Security Policy Press,
a division of the Center for Security Policy.

March 30, 2015

THE CENTER FOR SECURITY POLICY
1901 Pennsylvania Avenue, Suite 201 Washington, DC 20006
Phone: (202) 835-9077 | Email: info@securefreedom.org
For more information, please see securefreedom.org

Book design by Adam Savit
Cover design by Alex VanNess

"I charge you with five of what Allah has charged me with: to assemble, to listen, to obey, to immigrate and to wage Jihad for the sake of Allah"[1]

> - Quote from Hadith (five responsibilities or "charges" for those who submit to Islam)

We want to make it clear that we do not believe all refugees arriving in America are undeserving. The focus of our analysis is on the federal Refugee Resettlement Program and how it is being administered today with an eye to reforming it. It is critically important that it be administered with greater transparency than it has been to date---transparency for the US taxpayer and for the communities on the receiving end of the impact. Additionally, the numbers arriving and country of origin must be given greater scrutiny. Of course it is important that refugees are benefited from their opportunity to live in America, but of enormously greater consideration is whether the United States benefits from their presence.

---

[1] Sam Solomon and E Al Maqdisi, *Modern Day Trojan Horse: The Islamic Doctrine of Immigration* (Charlottesville, VA: ANM Publishers), 10.

TABLE OF CONTENTS

FOREWORD

Islamic doctrine holds that Mohammed is the perfect Muslim and, therefore, that emulation of his life is evidence of the highest level of devotion for the faithful. According to the sacred texts and traditions of Islam, Mohammed left his home town of Mecca in the 7th Century and traveled with a small band of followers to the city of Yathrib (now Medina), in what has become known as the hijra (migration). He did so with intent of establishing a new base of operations from which to conquer and rule.

Hijra remains the model to this day for jihadists who seek to populate and dominate new lands. Their migrations are not for the purpose of assimilating peacefully in a new host nation, adopting as their own its traditions and legal systems. Rather, Mohammed's followers, in keeping with the example established by their prophet, are driven first to colonize and then to transform non-Muslim target societies – whether through violent means or via stealthy, *pre*-violent ones favored by the Muslim Brotherhood when it is not powerful enough to use violence decisively.

Hijra forms a critical ingredient in what the Brotherhood calls its "civilization jihad." As its 1991 strategic plan entitled *The Explanatory Memorandum on the General Strategic Goal of the Group in North America* declares, the Brothers' mission in America is to wage civilizational jihad so as to "destroy the Western civilization from within." By aiming very explicitly at changing the demographics, legal systems and governments of such infidel states in an incremental process, the civilization jihadists advance their ultimate objective – global submission to shariah and the reestablishment of a caliphate to rule according to it.

Consequently, counterterrorism experts, other national security officials and politicians largely fixated on detecting and preventing attack from jihadist individuals or organizations are missing a no-less-important threat axis: the potential for subversion, as well as terrifying violence, from a Fifth Column in our country – fueled by rising numbers of immigrants, many of whom are brought here legally as refugees under America's dysfunctional immigration system. These dangers cry out, among other things, for reform of our refugee and asylum practices.

We are very pleased to be able to inform deliberations about the need for such reform and how it might best be achieved with this new monograph by Ann Corcoran, one of the country's foremost experts on the subject. Her Refugee Resettlement Watch website has, since its launch in 2007, become truly a go-to resource blog on this and related subjects. Ms. Corcoran's data and analysis suggest that, as presently operated, the U.S. government's Refugee Resettlement program is actually *exacerbating* the jihadist threat to our nation.

Particularly alarming is Ms. Corcoran's finding that the abdication of sovereignty with respect to the designation of refugees to the United Nations – an organization now largely governed by what some have called the proto-Caliphate, the Organization of Islamic Cooperation (OIC) – has led to a dynamic in which the asylum and refugee resettlement program is giving preferential treatment to problematic Muslim populations. Such cohorts typically adhere rigidly to the authorities of Islam's totalitarian and supremacist doctrine of shariah. They are, therefore, susceptible to domination and exploitation by Muslim Brotherhood organizations and operatives seeking to infiltrate and subvert unsuspecting Western societies "from within."

Matters are made worse by the blind spot that has been created with regard to this ideological wellspring of the Muslim Brotherhood and the Global Jihad Movement thanks to a systematic purge of all official U.S. government training curricula and vocabulary that might prove "offensive" to Muslims. Among the proscribed materials are *accurate* descriptions of the inspirational sources of Islamic terror to be found in the doctrine, law and scriptures of Islam.

One consequence of this willful blindness is that the federal immigration system welcomes increasing numbers of Muslim immigrants, asylum-seekers and refugees whose commitment to becoming true Americans is not even discussed, let alone systematically factored into decisions about who to admit. Moreover, as entire regions of the Middle East and other parts of the world descend into chaos, the ability of immigration officials to conduct proper vetting of applicants by verifying places of origin, political orientation, criminal records or even basic identity, is all too often non-existent.

The magnitude of the disaster being invited is, as Ms. Corcoran points out, evident in Western Europe where the results of misguided "multicultural" experiments, lax immigration policies and indifference to assimilation has produced entire neighborhoods in many countries that are essentially Muslim ghettos, where shariah prevails, outsiders rarely venture and even police and emergency responders need armed protection to carry out their duties. We are on notice, especially insofar as figures across the Islamic world – including the likes of Yousef al-Qaradawi (the senior jurist of the Muslim Brotherhood) and Anjem Choudary (the outspoken jihadist imam in the U.K.) – openly proclaim their intent to conquer the West from within through the process of Muslim migration.

This monograph, therefore, is most needed and timely. In it, as in the other volumes of the Center for Security Policy's Civilization Jihad Reader Series, the author is equipping the reader to understand the nature of an assault on our civil society institutions and governing agencies being mounted by Islamic supremacists in our midst. Having properly calibrated the threat, we then offer specific steps that can – and *must* – be taken to mitigate it.

At the outset of this assessment, it is important to emphasize that not all immigrants and refugees – and not even all Muslim immigrants and refugees – are undeserving of a chance at the American dream. We must recognize, however, that those who seek to subvert that dream certainly must not be afforded an opportunity to do so here.

This report is intended to encourage the reader to learn more about the federal immigration and refugee resettlement programs, and especially to be vigilant about serious shortcomings in the policies that govern such programs. The object is to prevent such defects from imposing alien populations on local communities while affording the latter little if any forewarning, time to prepare or opportunity to participate in the decision-making process. By equipping and empowering Americans at the local and state levels to rectify these unacceptable practices, we hope to minimize the danger posed by hijra to our country and to reconstitute a measure of national security-mindedness that is sorely needed throughout our polity.

Frank J. Gaffney, Jr.
President and CEO
Center for Security Policy

INTRODUCTION: WHAT IS THE HIJRA?

As more Americans lose sleep with worry about the next Islamic terrorist attack on America, whether from a "lone wolf" or organized Jihadist cells, we may be missing the most certain source of danger: the rise of Muslim migration through federal immigration policy including our refugee and asylum programs and other US immigration channels.

Hijra means *migration* and, according to Islam's doctrines and its quietly acknowledged organizational strategies, the goal of migration today is not peaceful assimilation to the political system and mores of the host country. Instead, the goal is jihad by *non-violent* means—known as *civilization jihad* or *Islamization.*

In an endorsement to Sam Solomon and E. Al Maqdisi's *Modern Day Trojan Horse: The Islamic Doctrine of Immigration,* Dutch political leader, Geert Wilders, put it succinctly: the vast settlement of Muslims in the West is bringing the *"gradual and incremental transformation of our societies and legal systems, or what is termed 'Islamisation' of our democratic societies by the vast growing numbers of Muslim immigrants who are importing Islam into our Western way of life."*[2]

Authors Solomon and Al Maqdisi call Muslim immigration to the West a *modern-day Trojan horse,* a giant, artfully crafted, hollow wooden horse statue, which hid a cadre of Greek soldiers. The Trojan Horse, made famous by the ancient epic poet Homer, was the means by which the citizens of Troy were persuaded to bring a belly full of shock troops from its long-warring enemy into the heart of their city.

The biggest sources of Muslim migration to the United States include the Refugee Resettlement/Asylum Program, as well as many other channels for legal and illegal immigration.

Jihad is a struggle against unbelievers. *Immigration is a jihad on the West.* It is a permanent jihad, creeping into every first world country, from the continent of Europe, to the Americas and to Australia and New Zealand. This jihad is happening

---

[2] Ibid, xiii

every single day in the steady drip, drip, drip of mostly legal Muslim migration into western Judeo-Christian societies from largely Muslim countries across the globe.

The most overlooked aspect of the increase in Muslim populations in the West, at least by the mainstream media, which prefers to fixate on the 'shiny objects' involving individual terror incidents and violent jihad, is the civilizational jihad in the U.S. (Europe too, of course).

In only the last two to three decades, Muslim immigration of Iraqis and Afghans from the Middle East, or Somalis from Africa, or Bosnians and Albanians from Eastern Europe, as well as the soon-to-be large scale Muslim migration from Syria (projected to begin this year in earnest), has burdened (or soon will burden) American communities with increasing demands for special treatment and sharia compliance as their populations grow and they become more *emboldened by the inexorable rise in their numbers.*

To see the writing on the wall and know we aren't making this up, we need only look to Europe, where the Muslim population is now large enough to be making demands. While Washington and the mainstream media engage in serial agonies over sensational incidents such as the Boston Marathon bombing or Oklahoma workplace throat-cutting, the Islamic migrants are *community organizing wherever they settle.* They are using our Constitutional freedoms and American good will to push a quiet form of jihad in towns and cities, large and small, right under our noses. Indeed, just because Fox News isn't reporting it, doesn't mean it's not happening.

Solomon and Al Maqdisi, in <u>Modern Day Trojan Horse</u>, suggest that those terrorist events actually dull our senses, conditioning us to be less shocked each time. These brave authors further suggest that, worldwide, the only difference in strategy between the violent jihadists and those working on building the Islamic state through migration and Islamic indoctrination is how much violence is the right amount at any given time, and how best to use any violence that does occur to their advantage.

Don't be distracted by terrorism, keep your eye on their long-term goal.

Is the *Hijra* reversible? Not likely. It might be slowed and better countered, however, but only if we see an immediate and dramatic shift in US immigration policy. And, given our weak Washington leadership at the dawn of 2015, this writer is not hopeful for much timely help from Washington.

Unlike a terror attack or a conflict somewhere in the world, which ends or is otherwise resolved at some point in time, once a Muslim population is established in a Western country or city, it is permanent.

Given this understanding, then, here are some of the things each of us can do to better deal with the situation:

- First, we must understand the threat and the Islamic doctrine that drives it.

- We must learn the structure and extent of immigration programs, like the US Refugee Resettlement Program.

- We must learn to identify and exploit gaps in the present policy to at least slow it down. Be brave (get tough-skinned about what they call you!).

- We must get engaged at the grassroots level, where Muslim activists are working locally.

- Finally we must put constant pressure on the mainstream media by competing with them through social media, alternative news outlets, and through individual investigative journalism projects to get the crucial message out: unchecked Muslim immigration will destroy us.

Our Constitutional right to free speech is our best weapon! So, don't be discouraged---use it!

Find your little piece of the battle and, to quote Winston Churchill, never, never give up.

MIGRATION IS JIHAD

In *Modern Day Trojan Horse*[3] Sam Solomon, a Christian convert from Islam and an expert on Islam, and his co-author E Al Maqdisi, tell us that Mohammad himself proclaimed that *migration is jihad.* As such, migration is a religious obligation. It is incumbent on all those believers who are able to migrate, from country to country, as well as from city to city, or town to town, to do so in order to build the Islamic state. Every day, they make advances in that agenda.

GEERT WILDERS' WARNING

After citing former Libyan leader Moammar Qaddafi's famous observation that Europe would be conquered without guns and swords, but with Muslim migrants over-running the Continent, Dutch Parliamentarian and leader of the Party for Freedom Geert Wilders, as we mentioned previously, said in his endorsement of _Modern Day Trojan Horse_:

> "... [O]ne can see that the threat from Islam doesn't just come in the form of Islamic terrorism by suicide bombers trying to wreak havoc in our cities. More often, **it comes in the form of gradual and incremental transformation of our societies and legal systems, or what is termed 'Islamisation' of our**

---

[3] Solomon and Al Maqdisi, *Modern Day Trojan Horse*, 14.

democratic societies by the vast growing numbers of Muslim immigrants who are importing Islam into our Western way of life.

Many in the West do not see the dangers that Islamisation poses to our civilization. Especially the ruling elite, who refuse to take action to counter Islamisation by prohibiting sharia Law, or to **take measures to regulate mass immigration.**"[4] [Emphasis added]

Wilders says it more clearly and with more authority than I can muster from having observed only a small but significant wedge of the Muslim migration process taking place in America over the last seven years.

ABOUT THIS REPORT

This report on Federal immigration policy, the Refugee Resettlement program, and the *Hijra* in America covers the following areas:

- It begins with a brief introduction to the Refugee Act of 1980 and defines some important terms.

- Next, it explores a few key elements of the *Hijra* as authors Solomon and Al Maqdisi describe it.

- The report then describes how I personally came to be involved with reporting on refugee resettlement and eventually became an advocate for limiting legal immigration.

- It then discusses some hard-to-pin-down numbers about the extent of Muslim immigration to America and the West, and takes a look at some of the Muslim ethnic groups gaining power in the US.

- The report undertakes a deeper analysis of the structure and function of U.S. Refugee Admissions Programs (RAP), especially the U.S. Refugee Resettlement Program that is helping, more than any other legal immigration program, to advance the Muslim migration.

- It describes the role of the United Nations High Commission for Refugees and details the major contractors (mostly church-based) that carry out our refugee programs using U.S. tax dollars and all too often, with an attitude that is surprisingly calloused.

- It further describes some questionable uses of refugee resettlement for other foreign policy purposes of the US government.

- It lists "preferred" cities for resettlement and reports on a recent phenomenon, the rise in "pockets of resistance."

---

[4] Solomon and Al Maqdisi, *Modern Day Trojan Horse*, xiii

Finally, the report considers what ordinary citizens can do to push back against the process of *Hijra*.

U.S. REFUGEE AND ASYLUM LEGISLATION

The Refugee Resettlement Program of the US State Department and the Department of Health and Human Services is now nearly 35 years old (2015 is the 35th anniversary of the *Refugee Act of 1980*).

It is important to note that there are other legal immigration avenues which are bringing tens of thousands of Muslims to our shores that are beyond the scope of this paper. For example, although Pakistanis comprise the largest number of Muslim immigrants arriving in America, many of them do not come as refugees. Doors were opened to Pakistanis in 1965 with the *'Immigration and Nationality Act'* of that year which eliminated quotas for Asian and African countries and allowed skilled and educated would-be immigrants to apply from all over the world. Family reunification (chain migration) also became a significant part of our immigration law.

The *Refugee Act of 1980* expanded the migration from Africa, the Middle East and Asia, but was aimed at another immigrant population---largely low-skilled and poorly educated "refugees," supposedly all fleeing persecution, who are in need of extensive government support. In the early days of the program, most were escaping Communism. Arguably the most attractive legal avenue to enter the US is as a "refugee" or successful asylum seeker because, in such cases, one is given a case worker to help secure employment and is immediately eligible for all forms of welfare.

It should be further noted that there is often confusion about the definition of a refugee and someone granted political asylum (an asylee). A refugee or asylum seeker must prove that he or she is persecuted for one of several reasons---political persuasion, religion, nationality or race---and cannot return safely to one's country of origin.

The difference between the two is how they reach America. A refugee is selected and screened abroad and flown here (at taxpayer expense), while an asylum seeker reaches our borders on his or her own steam and then asks for asylum to be granted. Once granted asylum, such migrants are called asylees and are given all of the social service benefits that refugees receive.

The so-called Somali Christmas Tree bomber was a refugee whose family was resettled in the Portland, Oregon area [5] while the Boston bomber family, often

---

[5] Jesse McKinley and William Yardley, "Suspect in Oregon Bomb Plot Is Called Confused," New York Times, 28 November 2010.
http://www.nytimes.com/2010/11/29/us/29suspect.html?pagewanted=1&_r=3&partner=rss&emc=rss&

referred to as "political refugees," had been granted asylum after arriving here on their own. [6] Both received protection and care under the *Refugee Act of 1980*.

THE U.S. TAKES THE LION'S SHARE OF THE WORLD'S REFUGEES

A 2012 UN report, the most recent one we could find, gives us a breakdown of the top countries of resettlement that year. The US tops the list with 50,097 followed by Australia (9,988), Canada (6,226), Sweden (2,044) and the UK (1,236). [7]

Now, have a look at the asylum applications for 2013 according to the UN High Commissioner for Refugees (UNHCR). In US law, asylum was originally envisioned (or so they said) to apply to only a small number of 'persecuted' people who managed to get to the US and apply for asylum status. An example would be a Russian ballet dancer seeking asylum after arriving in New York for a performance. Unfortunately, today asylum is outstripping the normal refugee process worldwide. In 2013 alone, the top five countries receiving asylum claims were led by Germany (109,600), USA (88,400), France (60,100), Sweden (54,300) and Turkey (44,800).[8]

In fact, Vernon M. Briggs, Jr., a professor of Economics at Cornell University, wrote in his incredibly thorough 2003 book, *Mass Immigration and the National Interest*, that asylum policy (formalized with the passage of the *Refugee Act of 1980*) has become the "Achilles heel" of our immigration system and has opened the doors to tens of thousands who can get to the US, enter the country and wait around, often for years, for approval.[9] I don't know that Professor Briggs could have envisioned ten years ago the scale of the abuse of asylum provisions of the 1980 Act that marked the border invasion in the summer of 2014.

UNACCOMPANIED CHILDREN AND THE DEFINITION OF ASYLUM

The political push to call the 'Unaccompanied alien children,' who arrived on our Southern border in great numbers during the summer of 2014, 'asylum seekers' is,

---

[6] "Janet Napolitano Defends Asylum Process Used By Boston Bombers' Family," Fox News Latino. 23 April 2013. http://latino.foxnews.com/latino/politics/2013/04/23/janet-napolitano-homeland-security-knew-boston-bomber-russia-trip/

[7] United Nations High Commissioner for Refugees, *Global Resettlement Statistical Report, 2012,* (UNHCR Regional Office, Washington DC), http://www.unhcr.org/52693bd09.pdf, 5

[8] United Nations High Commissioner for Refugees, *UNHCR report shows leap in asylum applications for industrialized countries,* http://www.unhcr.org/532afe986.html (March 21, 2014)

[9] Vernon M. Briggs, Jr., *Mass Immigration and the National Interest* (M.E. Sharpe, New York, 2003), 141

in this author's opinion, to expand the internationally recognized definition of the word "refugee" and apply it to anyone attempting to escape crime in their home country.

One can readily see that such an expansion of the definition would open us up to claims for asylum from all over the world--- requiring us to open our doors wide to those *fearing* basic criminal activity absent persecution---where their own government was unable or unwilling to protect them.

In addition to expanding the definition of "refugee," for the purposes of this report, one must be increasingly concerned with the OTMs (Other than Mexicans) crossing the border along with the "children." Indeed there are reports of Somali young men and women who cross the border and request asylum after making a journey that included stops in Russia and Cuba before reaching Central America; one wonders where they obtained the huge sums of money needed for a journey of that length and who was instructing them when they reached the US border.

OTHER LEGAL AVENUES FOR MUSLIM MIGRATION TO AMERICA

There are also myriad other legal opportunities to get into the US. There are visa programs, most notably student visas, tourist visas and investor visas (often abused by foreign nationals who get a foot in the door with such a visa and then file for asylum). But, you should know that among the top LEGAL avenues for permanent Muslim immigrant status (besides Refugee Resettlement) are the Diversity Visa Lottery and, to a lesser degree, a program called, ironically, Temporary Protected Status, that is anything but temporary.

Please have a look at the most recent 50,000 lucky winners of the Diversity Visa Lottery (often referred to as the Green Card lottery) and be prepared to be stunned at the number of Muslim countries on the list. Among the FY2015 "winners" are 517 Saudis.[10]

Those investor visas are also something that must be taken into greater consideration because evidence is building that some of the foreign nationals from Islamic countries who purchase small grocery stores and gas stations are funneling money out of the US through widespread fraud in our Supplemental Nutritional Assistance Program (food stamp system).

---

[10] US State Department, DV2015 Selected Entrants,
http://travel.state.gov/content/visas/english/immigrate/diversity-visa/dv-2015-selected-entrants.html

HOW MANY ENTERING THE U.S. ARE MUSLIMS?

As you will see in a later section of this report, we really don't have a good handle on the number. But for now, the Pew Forum on Religion and Public Life reported in 2013 that 1 million legal immigrants a year enter the US and 100,000 of them are Muslims,[11] and we will have to go with that rough number until such time as further research is done. For a point of comparison, Professor Briggs tells us that in 1980, as the Refugee Act was moving through Congress, the total number of all legal immigrants permitted to enter the US numbered just under 300,000.[12] In 2014 we are at a million and climbing.

Because of the US State Department's secrecy in reporting the number of Muslims arriving through the Refugee Admissions Program (RAP), we can only guess at how many Muslims are in the annual refugee pool based on which countries they hail from---30,000 is our best guess (this does not include the number who arrived here on their own and were granted asylum). More on those elusive numbers below.

Again, to guide your reading, after discussing Solomon and Al Maqdisi's Modern Day Trojan Horse, I'll tell you my personal experience with the Refugee Admissions Program and how I came to make the study of the program's impact a major calling.

We will discuss at some length how the program is administered and the major role played by so-called VOLAGs, short for Voluntary Agencies (non-governmental organizations), that are funded almost entirely by the US taxpayer and are, for all intents and purposes, running the show.

In subsequent sections, we will provide examples of the impact Muslim migration is having on communities, describe the community destabilization that often ensues, and identify "preferred" cities for resettlement. We will give a few examples of how the program has been abused for other foreign policy goals of the US government, resulting in increased Muslim migration to American cities.

In conclusion, we'll put forth a few ideas for what must be done to stop, or at least slow, the Muslim migration tide.

---

[11] Pew Research Religion and Public Life Project, *The Religious Affiliation of U.S. Immigrants: Majority Christian, Rising Share of Other Faiths,* http://www.pewforum.org/2013/05/17/the-religious-affiliation-of-us-immigrants/

[12] Briggs, *Mass Immigration,* 139

HIJRA, MIGRATION AND CIVILIZATION JIHAD

In our quote at the top of the report, we mentioned the Hadith. The Hadith are collections of traditions containing deeds and sayings of the Muslim prophet Muhammad. The Hadith and the *Sirat* (biographies of Muhammad) together comprise the Sunna and constitute a major source of guidance for Muslims, in addition to the Koran and sharia (Islamic Law). Readers here are very familiar with the five pillars of Islam, which sound relatively benign, but were you aware of the five charges (responsibilities) as discussed by Solomon and Al Maqdisi? One of those is to migrate.

Solomon and Al Maqdisi go on to explain that *migration is jihad* and is a "religious obligation"[13] for all those who follow Allah.

The authors cite Muhammad's *Hijra* as an example for all Muslims to emulate:

> Muhammad's Hijra, or migration from Mecca to Medina, is considered to be notably the most important Islamic event and is exemplified by the fact that the Islamic calendar starts with that event. For Hijra changed the status of Islam as a religion and of the Muslims as a community, transforming them from being a weak people to a powerful political entity, from being scattered groups of loyal individuals into a consolidated army, a united community and ultimately into a powerful socio-religious political state. [14]

HIJRA IS THE "MOST IMPORTANT METHOD OF SPREADING ISLAM..."

Solomon and Al Maqdisi emphasize again and again the primary goal of the Hijra:

> "....from the Islamic jurisprudence view the immigration of the Muslims to the West is to be regarded as the most important step on the ladder for achieving the establishment of an Islamic state in the West. This is the primary objective of Islamic mission in the West."[15]

They go on to explain that everything we see happening as the Muslim population grows is part of a carefully crafted and elaborate plan to bring about sharia and ultimately the complete domination of our government and society by Islamic Law.

To successfully dominate us, it is obvious that they need an ever-increasing number of Islamic adherents in order to carry out the next steps.

---

[13] Solomon and Al Maqdisi, *Modern Day Trojan Horse,* 3

[14] Solomon and Al Maqdisi, *Modern Day Trojan Horse,* 3

[15] Ibid, 36

For example:

Did you ever wonder why mosque-building was so important even as one might look around and see only a small population of Muslims in your community? The opening of mosques, first perhaps in storefronts, is to place a marker of sorts in a neighborhood which will then draw Muslims to the particular area (a mini-migration occurs) as they are encouraged to live near mosques.

As the attendance builds, skilled Imams work on the indoctrination of the worshipers. It is important that 'soldiers' in this jihad be well-versed, well-trained, and disciplined not only in the tenets of the 'religion,' but how to implement its societal and governmental goals in the broader community.

Ultimately the storefront mosque is replaced by an imposing edifice and public prayers follow, which let the community of *kuffars* (unbelievers) know, loud and clear, we are here!

To advance the quiet jihad, the teaching of Arabic is a critical requirement of the local mosque. Ultimately, pressure will mount on the local school system to make Arabic a part of the public school curriculum.

The top language of refugees resettled in America in the last seven years is Arabic (with Somali coming in at number four). [16] So, a ready-made population of Arabic speakers comes gratis the US State Department.

Muslims aggressively participating in the electoral process and running for public office is another important step. We saw how aggressive they could be in Minneapolis just as the 2014 election season got underway and a fight broke out at a political caucus between competing Somali contenders for political office. [17] The 2014 establishment of the USCMO (U.S. Council of Muslim Organizations), the first Muslim Brotherhood political party in the U.S., [18] likewise marked an important milestone in the civilizational jihad process.

Infiltration into all of our institutions, another phase of the takeover, is already well underway. Demands for Halal food, Islamic finance, and the visible presence of women in head scarves are all part of the plan to "condition the host community" as Solomon and Al Maqdisi point out.

---

[16] US State Department Refugee Processing Center, *Top 10 Languages Spoken by Arrived Refugees* (Posted Quarterly). http://www.wrapsnet.org/Reports/AdmissionsArrivals/tabid/211/Default.aspx

[17] Eric Roper, "Somali-Americans reflect on caucus chaos," *Star Tribune*, 6 February 2014. http://www.startribune.com/politics/statelocal/243874751.html?page=all&prepage=1&c=y#continue

[18] "Genesis of the U.S. Council of Muslim Organizations Muslim Brotherhood Political Party," *Center for Security Policy* (CSP), May 19, 2014. http://www.centerforsecuritypolicy.org/2014/05/19/genesis-of-the-us-council-of-muslim-organizations-muslim-brotherhood-political-party/

One of the clearest examples of the jihad of *Hijra* advancing in America is happening in Minnesota where the original "seed community" first resettled in Minneapolis is spreading to suburbs such as Eden Prairie, but also to St. Cloud farther north, where demands are now being placed on those communities (most recently demonstrated by a plan for a large mosque and school complex in a residential neighborhood). The US State Department opened a resettlement office in St. Cloud through Lutheran Social Services about ten years ago, and then subsequently began resettling Somalis directly from Africa to St. Cloud. A Muslim community sprang up in similar fashion in Rochester, MN.

The departure of dozens of young Minneapolis Somalis to join the jihadists in Africa and the Middle East is, despite some wishful thinkers who want to believe it is because they don't have enough jobs, 'resources,' and entertainment, is simply more evidence that Islamic indoctrination is going on in Minneapolis mosques.

In fact, a thorough study of the strategy unfolding in Minnesota would be of great value for confused citizens of other states who are just beginning to notice *something* happening, but holding the dangerously mistaken assumption that they are only disconnected events.

AUTHOR'S INTRODUCTION TO THE REFUGEE ADMISSIONS PROGRAM

My first introduction to the US State Department's Refugee Resettlement Program came in 2007.

Busy with life on a farm in rural Washington County, Maryland, raising children and running a non-profit horse rescue, I and some of my friends and fellow citizens became aware of something we thought was very unusual *at the time.*

Through the grapevine and then through one highly publicized event---the closing of a street in Hagerstown, our county seat, by hazmat-suited emergency workers who thought an African refugee living in a poor neighborhood of the city had Ebola---we learned that a "church" group from Virginia had been bringing several hundred refugees to the city.

How could that be? How is a church group---the Virginia Council of Churches---permitted to drop off refugees in a Maryland city? At first, we citizens only wanted to understand the governmental process and to learn who was paying for it, because it was very clear that at least some of the refugees (the Africans especially) were destitute, uneducated, and ill.

We also learned that a large group of the refugees were Meskhetian Turks (the Russian government did not want this Muslim minority group) being 'welcomed' to Hagerstown by the Islamic Society of Western Maryland (later to figure prominently in David Gaubatz and Paul Sperry's *Muslim Mafia*).[19] It was reported in our community that the Russian-speaking Meskhetians were being urged to learn Arabic at the Islamic center.

As of August 2007, 21,000 Meskhetians had applied for refugee status in America. I don't know how many ultimately were resettled, but I later heard that they

---

[19] P. David Gaubatz and Paul Sperry, *Muslim Mafia: Inside the Secret Underworld That's Conspiring to Islamize America* (Los Angeles, World Net Daily, 2009), 88-90.

were dispersed to 30 different US states. Ours had come (we were told through sources in the police department) because they were destined to be resettled in Lancaster, PA, where Church World Service (Virginia Council of Churches' senior partner) had an extensive resettlement program as a contractor of the US State Department, but Lancaster had, at about that time, reportedly experienced some refugee-related problems. I can only guess it was a hasty decision to send this group of Meskhetians to Hagerstown to take the pressure off of Lancaster. (Today Lancaster, home of the Amish people, is a "preferred" resettlement site and one of the most significant and culturally diverse sites for third world refugees in Pennsylvania.)

Having read works by authors Brigitte Gabriel, Nonie Darwish, Robert Spencer, Mark Steyn and in 2007, Ayaan Hirsi Ali, I was especially interested in the Muslim refugees arriving in our very conservative and rural county and wanted to know more about how this could be happening. So, I began my own inquiry. At first, as previously mentioned, I was largely driven by an interest in how this government program functioned, who was paying for it, and how it could be that "church" groups seemed in control of it.

It was Christine Brim (formerly Chief Operating Officer at the Center for Security Policy) who encouraged me to write a blog simply as a means of organizing and archiving what I learned about the program. *Refugee Resettlement Watch* became that website.

There were actually two events that occurred in 2007 that sent me on a quest for more information. One was the aforementioned resettlement of mostly Muslims to Washington County and the other was a little-noticed story in the *Washington Times* in August of that year.

In the summer of 2007, those of us questioning the program in Hagerstown, Maryland urged officials to hold a public meeting to explain to the citizens of Washington County how this resettlement plan would work. We had questions about taxpayer support---was the county completely responsible for housing, healthcare, education for the children? Where would the refugees work? Could we call a halt to the resettlement if the city became overloaded? Would the refugees be culturally comfortable in a rural 'red' county? Those were the questions foremost on peoples' minds. [20]

The public meeting was held on September 19, 2007 at Hagerstown Community College and those presenting information to the community came from all

---

[20] Ann Corcoran, "The Fix is in, Hagerstown Herald Mail does free publicity campaign for VCC," *Refugee Resettlement Watch*, 14 September 2007.
http://refugeeresettlementwatch.wordpress.com/2007/09/14/the-fix-is-in-hagerstown-herald-mail-does-free-publicity-campaign-for-vcc/

levels of government. The US State Department sent Terry Rusch, then Director of Refugee Admissions and Barbara Day, Domestic Resettlement Section Chief. Maryland's Office for Refugees and Asylees was represented, as was Church World Service (from the New York City headquarters office), and, of course, the Virginia Council of Churches.

In the audience was the chief of staff for Representative Roscoe Bartlett who represented the 6th Congressional District of Maryland at that time and who was well acquainted with Ellen Sauerbrey, a former Republican candidate for governor of Maryland, but who was, in 2007, serving as the Bush Administration's Asst. Secretary of State for Population, Refugees and Migration (PRM) in the US State Department and thus in charge of the entire refugee admissions program.

Those of us with questions about the local resettlement were lectured about how "America is a nation of immigrants" both from the stage and from some in the audience. For the most part, the local attendees in the auditorium were having none of it. I naively thought that the presenters would explain the program in detail, answer our questions, and that we could come to some accommodation about how many refugees would be resettled to the county in the future. However, it quickly became clear to concerned citizens that we were not getting straight answers.

Much to my surprise, ten days later, the announcement was made that the US State Department was closing the office in Hagerstown. The Virginia Council of Churches was sent back to Virginia with a parting shot at "unwelcoming" Washington County. I can only conclude that the US State Department wanted no further bad publicity out of the botched operation in western Maryland.

For those readers looking for more details, there is a good summary of the public meeting and the office closure at the *Emporia Gazette* by reporter Bobbi Mlynar. [21] At the time, Emporia, Kansas was having many problems with a large influx of Somali refugees who arrived to work for Tyson Foods, thus their interest in what was happening in Hagerstown.

To my knowledge there has not been another large public meeting with representatives from Washington and including all of their "stakeholders" in attendance (not just the supportive stakeholders but the critics as well) to explain to the community what is in store for them when a refugee office, contracted by the federal government, opens in a city.

---

[21] Bobbi Mlynar, "In Maryland, resistance closes refugee office," *The Emporia Gazette*, 28 November 2007, http://www.emporiagazette.com/news/article_2ce88f3c-6e8a-5b13-8810-6f08e4fde56b.html?mode=jqm

This past summer there was an abortive effort in Dover, NH to hold a public meeting to discuss the possible expansion of the over-loaded resettlement program from Manchester to nearby Dover, but as soon as word spread and public anger built, the meeting was quickly cancelled.

Unfortunately, once resettlement offices are up and running, they are rarely closed. Over the years, I've seen a few (Waterbury, CT comes to mind), but closures are usually only temporary and result most often from some misbehavior by the resettlement contractor.

30 MUSLIM MAYORS BY 2015

The second thing that focused my attention in the late summer of 2007 was an article in the *Washington Times*.

A month before our Hagerstown public forum on refugee resettlement, what caught my eye was a front page article in the *Washington Times* reporting on a trip by Imam Yahya Hendi to Saudi Arabia to speak with Saudi "academics."

At the time, Imam Hendi was the Muslim chaplain at Georgetown University and the Imam of the Islamic Society of Frederick, MD (Frederick is a city a half an hour east of Hagerstown). I had recalled seeing news stories in the local paper that Hendi had attended interfaith meetings in Washington County.

Promoted as a moderate voice, Hendi went to Saudi Arabia and said something quite improbable—*that the US would have 30 Muslim mayors by 2015!* Such a number might seem overly optimistic, but certainly was revealing in its intent.

Imagine if a Catholic or Jewish leader had made such a pronouncement, with the implication that they would somehow favor their co-religionists in the course of their governmental duties---we will have 30 Catholic mayors or 30 Jewish mayors by 2015---there would have been an uproar. Instead, Yahya Hendi's pronouncement went virtually unnoticed.

If Muslims were seeking to become part of the "fabric" of America, why did it matter if Muslims became mayors? Why wasn't anyone asking?

Here is a portion of that news item:

> RIYADH, Saudi Arabia — Muslims are steadily improving their position in U.S. society, contrary to the image of a community besieged by suspicions of links to militants, a leading U.S. Muslim cleric said yesterday.
>
> Yahya Hendi http://www.washingtontimes.com/topics/yahya-hendi/, a prayer leader who teaches at Georgetown University, said the September 11, 2001, attacks on U.S. cities spurred Americans to learn more about Islam and Muslims to affirm their U.S. identity. "I think the future is bright, because of

our wisdom in dealing with the reality," Mr. Hendi, a Palestinian by birth, said at a gathering of Saudi academics on a visit to Saudi Arabia.

"There are serious efforts being made among the second and third generation to become part of the political establishment. The challenge we face is in the media and from some Christian extremists who don't want an Islamic presence in America."

Mr. Hendi said U.S. Muslims were working on "nationalizing" Islam as part of the fabric of U.S. society, including cutting funding links to Muslim countries.

"Last year, we elected the first Muslim to Congress, and I expect that by 2015, there will be three or four, as well as at least 30 mayors," he said, adding that the number of Muslim lawyers in the United States has multiplied since September 11.

Islam has about 17,000 converts a year in the United States, but that is behind converts to Buddhism and evangelical Christianity, he said.[22] [Emphasis added]

Not enough converts? Who is counting converts? He doesn't say it, but what else is there to build a dominant voting population, to "nationalize" Islam if there aren't enough westerners heeding Allah's call and converting to Islam? Immigration, of course!

For more on Imam Hendi, see a discussion of Hendi as a paid speaker for the US State Department in testimony by Steven Emerson to the House Foreign Affairs Committee. [23]

See also Hendi's biography, which is now somewhat outdated. [24]

So to conclude this section, my interest in the Refugee Resettlement Program sprang from those two related concerns: The US State Department's resettlement of mostly Muslim Meskhetians as so-called refugees (so-called because these were not destitute people, but had homes to sell in Russia) in rural Washington County, MD in 2007 and the statements of an Imam (an internationally-known Islamic activist) from a nearby county who bragged to a Saudi audience that same year that they were working on installing 30 Muslim mayors in American cities, something they could only accomplish with a dramatic increase in a voting Muslim population.

---

[22] "Cleric Hopeful for US Muslims," *The Washington Times*, 6 August 2007. http://www.washingtontimes.com/news/2007/aug/6/cleric-hopeful-for-us-muslims/

[23] Steven Emerson, Investigative Project on Terrorism ,"Testimony before United States House of Representatives Committee on Foreign Affairs, Subcommittee on Terrorism, Nonproliferation, and Trade," 31 July 2008. http://www.investigativeproject.org/documents/testimony/357.pdf

[24] Imam Yahya Hendi, biography. http://www.imamyahyahendi.com/biography.html

MUSLIM POPULATION AT HOME AND ABROAD

I have found that it is extremely difficult to pinpoint exactly what the US Muslim immigrant population is at the present moment. Pew Research has several reports to help illuminate the controversial question.

In 2011 Pew put the total Muslim population in the US at 2.75 million (a large portion of that number is made up of Muslims who arrived as immigrants since 1992—1.7 million they say). [25]

Not surprisingly, the *Council on American Islamic Relations* (CAIR) thinks Pew is wrong and puts the US Muslim population at 7 million. This figure appears in a very useful report published by CAIR entitled *'The American Mosque 2011*[26] with handy maps including one depicting the Muslim population *"penetration"* by county. So, again, who is counting? They are!

The CAIR report which focused primarily on the growth in the number of mosques in America produced several major findings relating to the number of mosques and the relationship of the number to the size of the Muslim population. Claiming that 2.6 million Muslims attend Eid Prayer, they estimate a much larger 7 million total population:

> "If there are 2.6 million Muslims who pray the Eid Prayer, then the total Muslim population should be closer to the estimates of up to 7 million."[27]

---

[25] Pew Research Religion & Public Life Project, *The Religious Affiliation of U.S. Immigrants: Majority Christian, Rising Share of Other Faiths*, 17 May 2013. http://www.pewforum.org/2013/05/17/the-religious-affiliation-of-us-immigrants/

[26] Ihsan Bagby, Council on American Islamic Relations, *The American Mosque 2011*, January 2012. https://www.cair.com/images/pdf/The-American-Mosque-2011-part-1.pdf

[27] Ibid, 4

How they make that jump is questionable, but it is important to note that they are counting *their* people. As we said, one interesting map in the report depicts the county by county "Population Penetration" by Muslim adherents in the U.S. in 2010[28]. I doubt you could find any similar map for Christian or Jewish faith groups.

Above, we mentioned an important study by Pew Research on Religion and Public Life released in May 2013.

From that study, here are some of the estimates on the increase in Muslim immigration to America. Over a 20 year period from 1992 until 2012, Pew reports that the Muslim immigrant population has doubled. Since Pew claims that the total Muslim population in the US is about 2.7 million, the 1.7 million who entered in that one 20-year period is a significant portion of the present population.

> ...the estimated share of legal Muslim immigrants entering the U.S. each year has roughly doubled, from about 5% of legal immigrants in 1992 to about 10% in 2012. **Since 1992, the U.S. has admitted an estimated total of about 1.7 million Muslim immigrants.**
>
> [....]
>
> The estimated number of new Muslim immigrants varies from year to year but generally has been on the rise, going from roughly 50,000 in 1992 to 100,000 in 2012. **Since 2008, the estimated number of Muslims becoming U.S. permanent residents has remained at or above the 100,000 level each year.**
>
> [...]
>
> In recent years, a higher percentage of Muslim immigrants have been coming from sub-Saharan Africa. **An estimated 16% of Muslim immigrants to the U.S. in 2012 were born in countries such as Somalia and Ethiopia.** In 1992, only about 5% of new Muslim immigrants came from sub-Saharan Africa.[29] [Emphasis added]

Two years earlier, in 2011, Pew undertook a different study to attempt to predict the future growth of the global Muslim population by region of the world. For the Americas, here is what they said:

> Most of the projected growth in the region's (the Americas) Muslim population will take place in North America, particularly in the U.S. and Canada. If current trends continue, the Muslim population in the United States is projected to more than double in the next 20 years, from 2.6 million in 2010 to

---

[28] Ibid, 29

[29] Pew Research Religion & Public Life Project, *The Religious Affiliation of U.S. Immigrants: Majority Christian, Rising Share of Other Faiths*, 17 May 2013. http://www.pewforum.org/2013/05/17/the-religious-affiliation-of-us-immigrants/

6.2 million in 2030. Canada's Muslim population is expected to nearly triple, climbing from 940,000 in 2010 to 2.7 million in 2030.

[....]

The Americas is the only region where the percentage increase in the number of Muslims will be greater from 2010 to 2030 than it was from 1990 to 2010. From 1990 to 2010, the number of Muslims in the region increased by 2.3 million. In the next two decades, the number of Muslims in the Americas is projected to increase by 5.6 million. Much of the projected increase will come from the large number of Muslim immigrants expected to come to the U.S. and Canada from South Asia, the Middle East and North Africa.[30] [Emphasis added]

Another Pew study (at the Pew Research Center for the People & the Press) from later in 2011 (August), confirms what many have noticed in cities across America without actually counting heads--that most Muslim immigrants entered the US since 2000.

Most of the foreign-born Muslims came to the United States after 2000 (40%) or during the 1990s (31%). An additional 16% arrived in the 1980s. Just 12% arrived before 1980.[31] [Emphasis added]

Significantly, the Refugee Admissions Program came into existence in 1980 and correlates well with the significant uptick in Muslim migration to America.

That August 2011 study, geared toward reporters, entitled "Muslim Americans: No Signs of Growth in Alienation or Support for Extremism," offers us an opportunity for amusement. Pew asked Muslim respondents this question: "How much support for extremism is there among Muslim Americans?" and the percentage of those answering a "Great deal/fair amount" was 21%. Pew might conclude that shows little support for extremism, but when one considers there are at least, according to Pew, 2.7 million Muslims in America, that comes out to a whopping 567,000 of them who are thought to support 'extremism' to one degree or another!

60% of respondents said that they were very or somewhat concerned that there could be a possible rise in Islamic extremism in the US.[32] They must be basing that on something! What do they know that we don't? This same Pew study notes

---

[30] Pew Research Religion & Public Life Project, *The Future of the Global Muslim Population, Region: Americas*, 27 January 2011. http://www.pewforum.org/2011/01/27/future-of-the-global-muslim-population-regional-americas/

[31] Pew Research Center for People & the Press. *Muslim Americans: No Sign of Growth in Alienation or Support for Extremism, Section 1: Demographic Portrait*. 30 August 2011. http://www.people-press.org/2011/08/30/muslim-americans-no-signs-of-growth-in-alienation-or-support-for-extremism/

[32] Ibid

that some 65% of Muslims in America do not think of themselves first as Americans and only secondly as Muslims. On another question in the same survey, 33% of American Muslims stated their belief that there is only one interpretation of Islam.[33]

Incidentally, even Pew repeats a myth that the US State Department is happy to perpetuate

Pew repeats the misconception that the US State Department does not track the religious affiliation of refugees entering the US. To the contrary, I have recently found that all important data base kept at the State Department's Refugee Processing Center and it is a gold mine of information going back to 2002.

THE SOMALI POPULATION IN AMERICA

One ethnic group that Pew told us is growing rapidly, and one might think would be easier to track because they are virtually 100% Muslim, are the Somalis. But, the following points out how hard it is to get accurate numbers for just this one Muslim ethnic group in the US, largely because of reluctance by the Somalis to identify themselves and speak with a census taker.

At *Refugee Resettlement Watch*, we laboriously searched every *Office of Refugee Resettlement Annual Report* to Congress and were able to give exact refugee admission figures on the Somali immigration numbers going back to 1983 through the Refugee Admissions Program (these figures do not include, successful asylum seekers, Temporary Protected Status holders, Diversity Visa Lottery winners, other visa holders, or illegal aliens who have crossed into the US and not been apprehended.)[34]

- From 1983-1993 a total of 4,413 Somalis were admitted as refugees.

- From 1994-2001, the highest admission year was 2000 (6,002 Somalis) and the lowest admission year was 1995 (2,524).

- The number dropped precipitously in 2002 when fear spread that Somalis might harbor terrorists in the refugee population arriving from Africa. The total number admitted to the US was only 242.

- Then began the Bush years that saw the largest numbers arrive from a high of 12,814 (2004) to a low of 6,958 (2007).

- In 2008 the number dropped again because the US State Department discovered widespread fraud in the family reunification program for Africans

---

[33] Ibid

[34] Ann Corcoran, "How did we get so many Somali refugees?" *Refugee Resettlement Watch*, 10 September 2008. http://refugeeresettlementwatch.wordpress.com/2008/09/10/how-did-we-get-so-many-somali-refugees-the-numbers-are-telling/

(primarily Somalis) and closed that program for several years. The discovery and closure was reported by *Wall Street Journal* reporter Miriam Jordan in August of 2008.[35]

- Ultimately, the US State Department estimated that 20,000-30,000 entered the US illegally in the preceding decade, but no one was ever deported for the immigration fraud.

- Gradually, during the Obama years, the Somali refugee numbers have climbed steadily reaching 9,000 in FY2014.[36]

That brings the total number resettled through this one legal immigration avenue to 118,479 Somalis who have been busy for 30 years increasing their numbers through higher birthrates than those of Americans or other ethnic groups.

Just to show you how difficult it is to get a good estimate of numbers for various ethnic groups in America, however, a table from a US Census Bureau report for 15 major metropolitan areas and their African-born populations puts the total number of Somalis in major US cities at 76,205. We know from our research that 118,479 were actually admitted to the US as refugees over three decades. It defies logic that the Census Bureau puts the numbers so low. Where are they? Scattered across America in smaller cities, or not answering the doorbell?

The top three US Metropolitan areas, according to the US Census Bureau, for Somalis are in this order: Minneapolis (17,320), Columbus, OH (8,280), and Seattle (7,850); however, I expect the numbers are much higher because of trust and language problems related to Census gathering.[37]

A **USA Today** story in November 2014 about school integration problems in Eden Prairie, MN, involving the growing Somali student population there, puts the

---

[35] Miriam Jordan, "Refugee Program Halted As DNA Tests Show Fraud, Thousands in Africa Lied about Families To Gain U.S. Entry," *The Wall Street Journal*, 20 August 2008.
http://www.wsj.com/news/articles/SB121919647430755373?mod=googlenews_wsj&mg=reno64-wsj&url=http%3A%2F%2Fonline.wsj.com%2Farticle%2FSB121919647430755373.html%3Fmod%3Dgooglenews_wsj

[36] US State Department Refugee Processing Center, *Refugee Arrivals by Nationality,* 30 September 2014.
http://www.wrapsnet.org/Portals/1/Arrivals/Arrivals%20FY%202014/Arrivals%20by%20Nationality%20-%20Map%2810.6.2014%29.pdf

[37] U.S. Census Bureau, *Supplemental Table 1.Selected Countries of Birth for the United States and 15 Metropolitan Statistical Areas With the Largest African-Born Populations: 2008–2012.*
ftp://ftp2.census.gov/library/publications/2014/acs/acsbr12-16_supptabs.pdf

Somali population of the whole state of Minnesota at 32,000.[38] I expect further study will find that 32,000 is a low number.

We need to mention that Minnesota is the top state to receive 'secondary migrants.' That is a term used by the Washington professionals working in the refugee resettlement field. It means refugees who were resettled in one city, but who then move to another city usually to be with their own ethnic group (but sometimes for jobs, better welfare and affordable housing). Since it is so difficult to count the Somali population in the first place, we also doubt the accuracy of the secondary migrant numbers being compiled by the Office of Refugee Resettlement.[39]

THE ROLE OF BIRTH RATE

In the Pew study on the global Muslim population referenced earlier, researchers discuss at some length how they arrived at a Total Fertility rate of 2.5 children per Muslim woman living in the US, but fail to compare it to the birthrate of US non-Muslim women. They do make such a comparison for Canada:

> The fertility rate for Muslims in Canada is higher than the rate for other Canadians (an average of 2.4 children per woman for Muslims, compared with 1.6 children per woman for other populations in Canada). [40]

Consider also our previous discussion of how difficult it is to get accurate census information from Somalis, who we know anecdotally have large families, thus making any accurate prediction of fertility rates of Muslims versus non-Muslims an educated guess at best. Until we have more research, I would put US rates in the general vicinity of those in Canada (trusting to the Canadians' accuracy).

To confuse matters even more, this same 2011 Pew report on the Americas contains a graph which says that US Muslim immigration stood at 115,000 in 2010, which does not match the 2013 study referenced earlier that puts it at 100,000 annually, again pointing to a discrepancy in the numbers and the need for more demographic work on the Muslim population in America.

---

[38] "Diversity in the classroom—sides square off in Minnesota," *USA Today*, 25 November 2014 http://www.usatoday.com/longform/news/nation/2014/11/25/minnesota-school-race-diversity/18919391/

[39] US Dept. of Health and Human Services, Office of Refugee Resettlement. *Statistical Abstract for Refugee Resettlement Stakeholders*, July 2014, 9. http://www.acf.hhs.gov/sites/default/files/orr/statistical_abstract_for_refugee_resettlement_stakeholders_50 8.pdf

[40] Pew Research Religion & Public Life Project, *The Future of the Global Muslim Population, Region: Americas*, 27 January 2011. http://www.pewforum.org/2011/01/27/future-of-the-global-muslim-population-regional-americas/

Some demographers argue that, as immigrants become more prosperous, the size of their families declines; however, I would not count on that general rule necessarily holding up. Muslims may have reasons different than other Americans for producing large families---and that is to spread Islam.

Here we are at the end of a long discussion on Muslim immigration numbers in the US and the best we can do is to say that 100,000 to 115,000 Muslim permanent residents are admitted to the US every year. Clearly, serious demographic studies, in addition to those produced by Pew Research, are critically important.

MUSLIM POPULATION AROUND THE WORLD

We know that many European countries are experiencing enormous pressure to accommodate a growing Muslim population, larger even in total number, in some cases, than the US Muslim population, with its demands for Sharia law.

In an attempt to determine the tipping point, it is useful to have a look at some selected countries around the world where we know that pressure for sharia is intense and where a political backlash is underway.

Once again we must rely on a study from Pew Research and understand that its numbers are not set in stone, especially as it attempt to project forward to 2030.

Although it is helpful to compare the percentage of the Muslim population in the US to that in countries in Europe already experiencing demands for sharia compliance, there are many factors involved, especially as related to the degree of free speech permitted in each country and the willingness of its general population to push back on demands by Islamic activists to institutionalize their religious and political agenda.

Obviously, it does not require the population to be majority Muslim (by any stretch!) for the pressure to begin for sharia compliance, which are often, at first at least, of a very subtle nature. In fact, in the geographically vast United States (Australia too), the impact is being felt already in cities where the Muslim population has now grown to over 3% of the city's population, but is invisible to the majority of the country's citizens living in rural areas or in cities where the Muslim population is still tiny, largely because the mainstream national media are virtually silent in reporting trouble spots.

Making a broad generalization (from someone who doesn't pretend to have full grasp of the study of demographics), something seems to happen that emboldens a Muslim population when it approaches 3% of the population. We can quibble over the exact percent, but the point is, it is very low.

Coincidentally, this 3% figure is cited in that very important *Chicago Tribune* article, now ten years old, about the Muslim Brotherhood's early days in America. "Muslims make up less than 3 percent of the U.S. population, but estimates of their number vary widely from 2 million to 7 million."[41] Ten years ago, no one seemed to agree either on how many Muslims were in America!

Helping make the point, if officials are correct and the Census Bureau is wrong, Somalis represented about 5% of the population of Eden Prairie, MN as they began their public pressure to change the school system.

About 1,800 Eden Prairie residents claimed Somali ancestry on the latest U.S. Census survey, but city officials peg the number closer to 4,500 in a city of about 81,000.[42]

MUSLIM POPULATION BY COUNTRY

Don't look at Pew's numbers as the final word. Its accuracy as it projects forward to 2030 is greatly dependent on world events that have occurred since the numbers were published in 2011. Much has happened in the world in the last 3-4 years that has expedited Muslim emigration from the Middle East and Africa. The continuing crisis in Iraq and Syria, the so-called 'Arab Spring,' and the overthrow of Colonel Muammar Qaddafi in Libya have all contributed to a massive wave of migration only now hitting Europe.

In spite of Colonel Qaddafi's famous warning about how Europe would be conquered, not with guns and swords, but by an invasion of the Muslim migrant tide, reportedly he managed the flow out of Libya and toward Europe and had kept numbers in check from time to time. Since his 2011 overthrow (thanks to the work of Obama Administration officials including Secretary of State Hillary Clinton, UN Ambassador Susan Rice and White House advisor Samantha Power), the country has descended into chaos and there has been a swelling tide of migrants coming out of Libya, as well as other North African countries, and trying to sail to Europe on unseaworthy vessels.

A relevant fact that should not be forgotten is that current UN Ambassador Samantha Power began her career in the Obama White House as the Iraqi Refugee Czar, whose job it was to open the spigot and move Iraqis into American cities. As

---

[41] Noreen S. Ahmed-Ullah, Sam Roe and Laurie Cohen, "A rare look at secretive Brotherhood in America," *Chicago Tribune*, 19 September 2004, http://www.chicagotribune.com/news/watchdog/chi-0409190261sep19-story.html#page=1

[42] "Diversity in the classroom—sides square off in Minnesota," USA Today, 25 November 2014 http://www.usatoday.com/longform/news/nation/2014/11/25/minnesota-school-race-diversity/18919391/

the Obama adventure in Libya got underway, the Soros-protégé was quoted as saying she was tired of doing "rinky-dink do-gooder" stuff. [43]

Also, to further disrupt Pew's predictions for 2030, most notably Germany and Sweden have (since 2011) thrown wide their doors to Muslim asylum seekers from Syria, Iraq, Somalia, and Afghanistan. Other countries such as Malta, Greece, and Italy, at the Mediterranean edge of the European Union, have seen their countries overwhelmed with Syrians, Somalis, Libyans, and even Egyptians, among others, arriving on boats provided by human traffickers.

As a result, Pew's projected percentage increase in the Muslim population for countries including Malta and Italy are definitely now way off base.

We don't have time to go any deeper, but readers should be aware of the fact that the US State Department has, since 2007, been taking hundreds of mostly Somali aliens (who arrived in Malta illegally) to the US as "refugees" in complete disregard of normal international refugee resettlement practices.

Here are some selected countries from the Pew Table on Muslim Populations by Country. [44] For those of you who have been observing the civilization jihad in Europe, you will readily see the correlation between numbers and public anxiety levels (and the political backlash against further immigration from Muslim countries) experienced by the citizens of certain countries:

---

[43] Ann Corcoran, ""White House's Power: "Doing rinkey-dink do-gooder stuff,""" *Refugee Resettlement Watch*, 31 May 2012. http://refugeeresettlementwatch.wordpress.com/2012/05/31/white-houses-power-doing-rinkey-dink-do-gooder-stuff/

[44] Pew Research Religion and Public Life Project, "Table: Muslim Population by Country," 27 January 2011. http://www.pewforum.org/2011/01/27/table-muslim-population-by-country/

Country	Muslim population by % 2010	Muslim population by % 2030 (projected)
Argentina	2.5	2.6
Australia	1.9	2.8
Austria	5.7	9.3
Belgium	6.0	10.2
Bulgaria	13.4	15.7
Canada	2.8	6.6
Denmark	4.1	5.6
France	7.5	10.3
Germany	5.0	7.1
Greece	4.7	6.9
Ireland	0.9	2.2
Italy	2.6	5.4
Malta	0.3	0.3
Netherlands	5.5	7.8
Norway	3.0	6.5
Poland	0.1	0.1
Russia	11.7	14.4
Spain	2.3	3.7
Sweden	4.9	9.9
US*	0.8	1.7
UK	4.6	8.2

* Pew's projected 2030 Muslim population total for the US is 6,216,000, which is below what CAIR claimed it had already reached in 2011 (about 7 million) or that was being promoted by Muslim activists in 2004.

Note that none of the countries of interest are declining in Muslim population as a percentage of the overall population. And, although focusing mostly on Europe, we included Argentina because the Muslim migration is not only underway in Europe, Australia and North America, but is spreading into South America as well.

It appears that Mark Steyn was correct in his important work, *America Alone: The end of the world as we know it!*[45] We are alone (except for maybe Poland!).

If we wish to avoid the sorts of societal disruptions now being experienced in such formerly complacent-while-homogeneous locales such as Sweden, it is imperative that we understand the implications of surpassing that 3% Muslim population level while failing to ensure appropriate assimilation and integration into the broader American society. But how?

Unfortunately, working against us every day to increase the Muslim population in America is the *US Refugee Admissions Program and the 'non-profit' organizations that hold federal contracts to resettle refugees.*

---

[45] Mark Steyn, *America Alone: The end of the world as we know it* (Washington, DC: Regnery Publishing Inc., 2006)

HOW THE REFUGEE ADMISSIONS AND RESETTLEMENT PROGRAM WORKS

One thing I can say unequivocally is that the program created by the *Refugee Resettlement Act of 1980* has been steeped in secrecy for the last 30 of its nearly 35 years, so it is no wonder it has escaped scrutiny.

It is only in the last five years or so that we have learned about some basic elements of the program that is run jointly between the US State Department, the Department of Health and Human Services (Office of Refugee Resettlement), and the Department of Homeland Security. To borrow a phrase, it has just recently begun to come out of the shadows.

Not surprisingly, seven years after its arrival in Washington County, Maryland, we still learn new things every day.

Incidentally, this past summers' crush of "unaccompanied alien children" claiming asylum at our southern border has done more to put the word "refugee" into the American lexicon than any other single event in years. Unfortunately now, in many American homes, the word "refugee" likely carries a negative connotation.

The refugee influx has been largely ignored by the major immigration control groups, perhaps due to the fact that some of those leading groups (Federation for Immigration Reform, Center for Immigration Studies, and Numbers USA) have been so focused on *illegal* immigration that the legal Refugee Admissions Program (RAP) with its relatively smaller numbers of immigrants, and the aura built up around the word "refugee" by its proponents and the media in general, have helped it to slip under the radar.

Because we are choosing refugees from cultures alien to the Western Judeo-Christian ethic, it makes the refugee program, despite its smaller size, perhaps more impactful than the arrival of larger numbers of Hispanic Christian illegal aliens might be on a community. Although we shouldn't be making broad generalizations, it is only common sense that Christian Spanish-speaking immigrants are going to more quickly adopt our cultural ways than, say, a Burmese Muslim might. Plus, they aren't being taught in a mosque about the importance of staying separate from the *kafir* (infidel) population.

Also making the program powerful in changing the demographic make-up of some communities is the fact that US government policy aids in the building of ethnic/religious enclaves in smaller cities in addition to the usual traditional and historic gateway cities one expects.

Solomon and Al Maqdisi in *Modern Day Trojan Horse* emphasize the need for Muslims to stay segregated in order to consolidate their position and press their demands on the host society.

> "The first foundational principle for the creation of a successfully visible Islamic Society is to be **separate** and **distinct**." [Emphasis in the original].[46]

So, in an age when we are told that multiculturalism is to be revered, some Muslim refugees are not even attempting to assimilate and federal government policy and funding actually encourage and reward ethnic and religious separation.

Here is an example:

Increasingly, the impact of the large numbers of refugees arriving in the US is being felt in cities large and small as certain ethnic and religious groups colonize neighborhoods and seem impervious to any message to assimilate and truly become Americans who fully accept our Constitution and rule of man-made law. It isn't just the individual immigrants themselves who are resisting (Somalis come immediately to mind) and who are for the most part choosing enclaves in cities such as Minneapolis, Columbus, Seattle or even the much smaller Lewiston, Maine, in which to live with their own people, but the Office of Refugee Resettlement (Health and Human Services) is in fact awarding federal grants which encourage separation of the various nationalities admitted.

It will probably come as a shock to readers to learn that federal taxpayers fund millions of dollars in grants to so-called Ethnic Community Based Organizations (now called Ethnic Community Self Help organizations). Here (below) are some of the recent grants awarded for what amounts to little ethnocentric ACORN-like community organizing centers which teach their people, their ethnic group members, in selected cities, how to access social services, gain citizenship, vote and speak politically when the need arises.

If indeed there is a need in a given community for guidance to refugees on where to access their social services or address other needs on their paths to citizen-

---

[46] Solomon and Al Maqdisi, *Trojan Horse,* 18

ship, why aren't we using the existing resettlement agencies (the VOLAGs) and tasking them with a multicultural approach to their help? We already employ resettlement contractors (to be discussed in greater detail below) in all of these cities who should be doing this work in a multicultural fashion as part of their contract with the US State Department and their work with the Office of Refugee Resettlement.

Here are just a few on-going federal grants to Ethnic Community Self-help groups that should surprise you:

- Association of Africans Living in Vermont, Burlington ($125,000)

- Somali Cultural and Development Association, Portland, ME ($150,000)

- Iraqi Mutual Aid Society, Chicago ($185,000)

- Arab Community Center for Economic and Social Services, Dearborn, MI ($175,000)

- Somali Family Services, San Diego ($179,823)

- Iraqi American Society of Peace and Friendship, Phoenix, AZ ($194,404)

Those are just six of the 38 grants on-going as of this writing at the Office of Refugee Resettlement (ORR) totaling millions of your tax dollars to promote separation rather than assimilation.[47]

STRUCTURE OF THE REFUGEE ADMISSIONS PROGRAM

Chief proponents of what ultimately became the *Refugee Act of 1980* (signed into law on March 17, 1980 by President Jimmy Carter) included lead sponsor Senator Ted Kennedy of Massachusetts and then-Senator Joe Biden of Delaware. Other Senators promoting the bill as it went through the Senate included a who's who of Democratic Senators of the period.

Those in Congress expressing concerns about importing poverty wanted to know how many refugees (remember, at the time, the Cuban and Vietnamese boat people were foremost on peoples' minds) the US was taking compared to other developed countries. Once assured we were not taking the largest number of Vietnamese refugees, opposition by Senator Strom Thurmond disappeared and the bill passed the

---

[47] US Dept. of Health and Human Services, Office of Refugee Resettlement, *Ethnic Community Self-Help Grants FY2014/2015*. http://www.acf.hhs.gov/programs/orr/resource/ethnic-community-self-help-grants

Senate by a vote of 85-0, according to a report authored by Senator Ted Kennedy in 1981.[48]

Interestingly, the Act capped the number of refugees that would be admitted at 50,000 until 1983, and thereafter the limit could only be increased by the President *after* consultation with Congress. In an emergency, the President can admit additional refugees, again, *"after appropriate consultation with Congress."*

Perhaps the law has been amended at some point in the last 30 plus years (an exhaustive review is beyond the scope of this paper), but today Congress appears to have completely given up any role in the selection and number of refugees admitted to the US to the wishes of the US State Department, which is following the marching orders of the United Nations High Commission Commissioner for Refugees (UNHCR).

The President, in the closing weeks of September each year, sends a 'Presidential Determination,' largely prepared by the State Department, to the appropriate committees in Congress: to my knowledge, those committees rubber-stamp whatever the President sends to them. The public cannot attend the briefing (we have tried).

According to Briggs, in his exhaustive review of mass immigration to America, Congress is "required to hold a hearing on the number."[49]

A hearing! As far as we know, what the President sends up to the Hill is never even questioned.

In recent years the "ceiling" has been set at 70,000 refugees per year hailing from upwards of 70 countries (that does not include those tens of thousands granted asylum, victims of human trafficking, or the sky-rocketing numbers of 'Unaccompanied Alien Children' that come under the care of the Office of Refugee Resettlement in the Department of Health and Human Services).

In fact, in summarizing Fiscal Year 2013 responsibilities, ORR Director Eskinder Negash reported that they cared for 143,000 arrivals from 65 countries, and, including, in addition to the "refugees," a whole host of other categories of legal immigrants.[50]

---

[48] Edward M. Kennedy, "Refugee Act of 1980," *International Migration Review* © 1981 The Center for Migration Studies of New York, Inc., Vol. 15, No.1/2
http://www.jstor.org/discover/10.2307/2545333?uid=3739256&uid=2&uid=4&sid=21105433785843

[49] Briggs, *Mass Immigration*, 140

[50] US Dept. of Health and Human Services, Office of Refugee Resettlement, *Office of Refugee Resettlement Year in Review—FY2013*, 20 December 2013. http://www.acf.hhs.gov/programs/orr/resource/office-of-refugee-resettlement-year-in-review-fy2013

At the present time, there is a lobbying campaign underway by NGOs such as the Hebrew Immigrant Aid Society and the International Rescue Committee (two of nine major State Department refugee contractors/VOLAGs to be discussed further below) to increase this year's (FY2015) ceiling to 100,000 to accommodate a wish list of 15,000-30,000 Syrians to be admitted to the US from UN camps.[51] Sunni Muslims are the dominate group living in UN camps, so it stands to reason that most of the Syrians who have already begun arriving in the US are Muslims.

THE STATE DEPARTMENT DISCOUNTS PUBLIC OPINION

In preparing the Presidential Determination 'letter' to Congress (Obama Presidential Memorandum)[52] and the accompanying report to Congress[53], the US State Department takes public testimony on the "size and scope" of the plan for the upcoming year.

Five years ago those public "scoping" meetings were dominated by refugee contractors whose obvious interest is in admitting more refugees since the size of their State Department contract is dependent on the number of refugees they resettle (they are literally paid by the head).

Then, at *Refugee Resettlement Watch*, we began announcing the public comment period and citizens concerned with the numbers and the ethnic/religious make-up of the Refugee Admissions Program began to submit testimony. Some attended the "hearing" in person (the only public session was in the Washington, DC area). Those of us who attended in person were given access to the entire stack of testimony submitted (in hard copy, not electronically). We quickly saw that the critics of the program were now outnumbering the supporters, who were largely limited to those individuals and organizations with a vested financial and political interest in seeing more refugees resettled.

---

[51] Ann Corcoran, "Hebrew Immigrant Aid Society Launches Petition Drive," *Refugee Resettlement Watch*, 29 October 2014.

http://refugeeresettlementwatch.wordpress.com/2014/10/29/hebrew-immigrant-aid-society-launches-petition-drive-to-increase-this-years-refugee-quota-from-70000-100000/

[52] White House Press Release, *Presidential Memorandum---FY2015 Refugee Admissions*, 30 September 2014. http://www.whitehouse.gov/the-press-office/2014/09/30/presidential-memorandum-fy-2015-refugee-admissions

[53] US State Department, Bureau of Population, Refugees and Migration, *Proposed Refugee Admissions for Fiscal Year 2015*, 18 September 2014. http://www.state.gov/j/prm/releases/docsforcongress/231817.htm

So the public scoping meeting in Washington in 2013[54] was dominated by critics, when only two years prior to that, the meeting room was filled with those "stakeholders" pushing for more refugees, including much to this writer's shock, the US Conference of Catholic Bishops (one of nine major federal contractors) which *was asking for more Rohingya (Burmese) Muslims to be admitted to the US*

We wonder if the horrific death of a little Christian girl in Salt Lake City, Utah in 2008 gave Catholic Charities, a resettlement contractor in Utah, a moment's pause. Esar Met, a Burmese Muslim, was convicted and sentenced in May 2014 to life in prison for the rape and murder of 7-year-old Hser Ner Moo.[55]

A reporter for the *Salt Lake Tribune* travelled to Thailand and learned that the Christian Burmese and the Muslims (including Esar Met) were kept in separate sections of the camps.[56]

In Salt Lake City, apparently not understanding the centuries-old animosity between Thai Muslims and Christians, or the incidence of Muslim attitudes of license towards non-Muslim women and girls, a refugee agency placed Met in a Christian-dominated apartment complex where he killed the little girl reportedly within weeks of his arrival in the US.

Back to the State Department scoping meeting....

Perhaps unhappy with the growing public opposition to refugee resettlement, the State Department held no public hearing at all in 2014 (to prepare the FY2015 Presidential Determination). *The U.S. State Department took 'testimony' electronically, but no one outside the system was allowed access to any of it.*

THE REFUGEE ACT OF 1980

In the years leading up to the passage of the *Refugee Act of 1980*, the US took in over 100,000 Vietnamese refugees who were cared for by churches and other civic groups throughout America on a family-by-family/church-by-church basis. There was no complex system for resettlement yet established and few if any resettlement contractors as we know them today were hired as federal contractors; nevertheless, by

---

[54] Ann Corcoran, "You did it! Your testimony flooded State Department hearing yesterday," *Refugee Resettlement Watch,* 16 May 2013. http://refugeeresettlementwatch.wordpress.com/2013/05/16/you-did-it-your-testimony-flooded-state-department-hearing-yesterday/

[55] Ben Winslow, *"Esar Met sentenced in 7-year-old's murder,"* Fox 13 Salt Lake, 14 May 2014, http://fox13now.com/2014/05/14/esar-met-sentenced-in-7-year-olds-murder/

[56] Julia Lyon, *"Stolen hope: Daughter's death comes after years of fear, running for a Burmese family,"* Salt Lake Tribune, 31 March 2008, http://extras.sltrib.com/thailand/chapter1.html

most accounts, the refugees were taken in and successfully started on their lives as new Americans.

For further research at a later date, an effort should be made to uncover just who proposed the scheme to create a "public-private partnership" between the federal government and non-governmental organizations, so-called "religious charity" groups (and a few secular ones), that now monopolize all refugee resettlement in America.

It may have sounded like a good idea at the time, but the public-private partnership envisioned (or at least hoped for by some who voted for the new law) by the designers of the *Refugee Act* has become meaningless as the public share of responsibility has grown dramatically while the private share has virtually dried up. Or, was that the plan all along?

Before supporters of the present monopolistic system raise the issue of all of the volunteers working in the 180 cities, one should be aware of the fact that there is even a "match" plan which allows contractors to log volunteer hours and then receive cash compensation from the federal treasury for the time contributed by volunteers.

In the original Kennedy/Biden/Carter law, $200 million in federal funds was authorized annually for non-profit organizations and state and local government to help the refugees get settled, find jobs and become self-sufficient. No one in his right mind would have voted for a bill that would have simply opened a pipeline of poverty into America, but that is what has happened.

The Act also set up a complicated sharing of responsibility among three separate administrative agencies of government, making it very difficult to pin down the costs and duties of all those involved. Simply put, *the Department of Homeland Security screens prospective refugees abroad* and the *US State Department admits the refugees to the U.S. and contracts and provides funding to non-governmental organizations (VOLAGs to be discussed below) to place them in cities across the country. The Department of Health and Human Service's Office of Refugee_Resettlement (ORR) funds the State Department's contractors for myriad other needs and activities involving the resettled refugees.*

In that most recent FY2015 report to Congress, we learn that the basic federal outlay (to resettle 70,000 refugees) to the three cabinet-level departments has mushroomed to over a billion dollars:

Estimated Available Funding For Refugee Processing, Movement, And Resettlement

FY 2014 and FY 2015 ($ Millions)

Agency	Estimated FY 2014 (by Department)	Estimated FY 2015 (by Department)
Refugee Processing Department of Homeland Security *United States Citizenship and Immigration Services*	$32.3	$32.9
Refugee Admissions Department of State *Bureau of Population, Refugees and Migration*	$494.4	$418.0
Refugee Resettlement Department of Health and Human Services *Administration for Children and Families, Office of Refugee Resettlement*	$616.3	$608.1
Total	$1,143.0	$1,059.0

The estimated FY 2015 figures above reflect the President's FY 2015 Budget request and do not include carryover funds from FY 2014.

Please see the entire report for additional clarification on the numbers: Proposed Refugee Admissions for FY2015[57]

---

[57] US State Department, Bureau of Population, Refugees and Migration, *Proposed Refugee Admissions for Fiscal Year 2015*, 18 September 2014. http://www.state.gov/j/prm/releases/docsforcongress/231817.htm

Consider the fact that the above numbers do not include the costs for the bloated SNAP program (food stamps), subsidized housing, most health care, educational costs for the children, and costs associated with the criminal justice system including translators required by a Clinton-era executive order. *Those additional costs must be absorbed by local and state government, thus presenting a major Constitutional question regarding states' rights that has not ever been legally challenged to this writer's knowledge.*

THE FEDERAL CONTRACTORS WHO RUN THE SHOW

Presently, there are nine non-governmental organizations, six 'religious charities' and three secular ones, which monopolize federal grants and contracts for placing refugees in 180 (and counting) cities across America. Working for the top nine major NGOs are 350 subcontractors, which makes 'following the money' exceedingly challenging to say the least.

The Office of Refugee Resettlement calls the nine---VOLAGs---short for Voluntary Agencies,—which is a joke considering the fact that all of them are largely funded by the US taxpayer. They all resettle Muslim refugees and I have never seen any public statement from any of them about saving the Christians and other minorities of the Middle East as a *first* priority.

In fact, the responsibility for the large Somali population in Minnesota can be laid at the feet of Catholic Charities, Lutheran Social Services, and World Relief.

All of these 'non-profit' groups (VOLAGs), in addition to advocating for more refugee resettlement, lobbied for the Senate-passed *S.744 Comprehensive Immigration Reform bill* which includes an expanded role for them in serving the newly-amnestied aliens. Additionally, some listed below have boosted their federal income in recent years with grants and contracts to care for the 'Unaccompanied alien children' flooding our Southern border.

- Church World Service (CWS)

- Ethiopian Community Development Council (ECDC) (secular)

- Episcopal Migration Ministries (EMM) (Officially: The Domestic and Foreign Missionary Society of the Protestant Episcopal Church in the USA)

- Hebrew Immigrant Aid Society (HIAS)

- International Rescue Committee (IRC) (secular)

- US Committee for Refugees and Immigrants (USCRI) (secular)

- Lutheran Immigration and Refugee Services (LIRS)

- United States Conference of Catholic Bishops (USCCB)

- World Relief Corporation (WR)

Church World Service, the parent organization of the Virginia Council of Churches, first brought my attention to the Refugee Admissions Program. In fact, a top official from Church World Service came to Hagerstown, MD from New York City on June 12, 2007 to meet with me in hopes of assuaging my concerns about the program.

In the course of the meeting, an old news clipping was produced about a 2006 KKK demonstration at the Antietam Battlefield adjacent to our family farm. The senior official was clearly attempting to implicate me (maybe our whole rural community) as racist and bigoted, simply because some insignificant KKK group had chosen the site of Lincoln's inspiration for drafting the Emancipation Proclamation at which to hold a demonstration. Infuriated as we were by the insinuation being made, the character of those seeking to flood our community with needy people was re-vealed---these were hardened Leftists, not exemplary and kind-hearted Christians.

Refugee resettlement has become a major money-maker for what can only be described as the "Religious Left," whose goal is to change the demographic make-up of the 180-plus cities and towns in which they presently work.

To give readers some idea of the federal dollars involved, below is a break-down based on the most recent financial reports or Form 990's available for the top nine VOLAGs, which are paid (by the head) by the U.S. State Department to resettle refugees. They are then awarded additional grants and contracts by the Office of Ref-ugee Resettlement (Dept. of Health and Human Services). The system is set up in such a way that there is no incentive to slow the flow because the VOLAG/contractors have offices to run and staff to pay.

In fact, in a very slow resettlement year following 9/11 (slow for fear of ter-rorists using the program), the federal agencies managed to continue funding the VOLAGs as if the refugee arrival rates were still at a pre-9/11 level.

Federal funds flow through the nine to their subcontractors for everything from English language programs to grants for refugee gardens and healthy marriage training programs. They also manage special federally-matched savings accounts for refugees and micro-enterprise loans for business start-ups for their refugee "clients."

One enterprise encouraged by federal grants is the training of day care work-ers who will provide child care which serves yet further separation instead of assimilation. The ORR says they train refugees who will provide children in their care with "appropriate cultural competency" in their home-based childcare businesses.[58] So why aren't they encouraged to take care of children in *multicultural* day care facilities that promotes the English language?

CHURCH WORLD SERVICE

- (From 2012 Form 990)
- Total revenue: $76,185,774
- Govt. grants and contracts: $45,431,781
- Percent taxpayer funded: 60%
- Top salary: $286,000 (Top salaries include benefits and income from related activities)

ETHIOPIAN COMMUNITY DEVELOPMENT COUNCIL

- (From 2012 Form 990)
- Total revenue: $15,244,802
- Govt. grants: $14,609,687
- Percent taxpayer funded: 96%
- Top salary: $233,228

EPISCOPAL MIGRATION MINISTRIES

This gets tricky. Apparently EMM (or now known as Domestic and Foreign Missionary Society of the Protestant Episcopal Church of America), does not produce a Form 990 (no response from them to a recent inquiry was received) nor do they publish their federal income in their annual report.

The only accounting we could find is an independent auditor's report that reveals they received $17,365,325 from the federal government for their refugee program in 2012.[59]

---

[58] US Department of Health and Human Services, Office of Refugee Resettlement, *About Home Based Child Care*. http://www.acf.hhs.gov/programs/orr/programs/microenterprise-development-hbcc/about

[59] Consolidated Financial Statements and OMB Circular A-133 Supplementary Information Together with Reports of Independent Certified Public Accountants, *Domestic and Foreign Missionary Society of the Protestant Episcopal Church of the USA,* 31 December 2012 and 2011. 30.
http://www.episcopalchurch.org/sites/default/files/downloads/dfms_-_omb_a-133_12-31-12_report.pdf

Further examination by a qualified accountant would be needed to find out how they spent the $17 million.

HEBREW IMMIGRANT AID SOCIETY

- (From 2012 Form 990 for HIAS, Inc. Can't be found at *Guidestar* under its full name, but only as HIAS, Inc, just one of those things that makes tracking these VOLAGs very difficult)

- Total revenue: $25,418,714

- Govt. grants and contracts (including travel loan income): $15,426,116

- Percent taxpayer funded: 61%

- Top salary: $323,162

INTERNATIONAL RESCUE COMMITTEE

- (From 2012 Form 990)

- Total revenue: $456,122,865

- Govt. grants and contracts (including travel loan income): $332,271,151

- Percent taxpayer funded: 73%

- Top salary: $485,321

US COMMITTEE FOR REFUGEES AND IMMIGRANTS

- (From 2012 Form 990)

- Total revenue: $39,205,548

- Govt. grants and contracts: $38,817,939

- Percent taxpayer funded: 99%

- Top salary: $289,192

LUTHERAN IMMIGRATION AND REFUGEE SERVICE

- (From 2012 Form 990)

- Total revenue: $43,563,804

- Govt. grants and contracts: $42,047,935

- Percent taxpayer funded: 97%

- Top salary: $214,237

WORLD RELIEF (NATIONAL ASSOCIATION OF EVANGELICALS)

- (From 2012 Form 990)

- Total revenue: $56,842,649

- Govt. grants and contracts: $38,837,294

- Percent taxpayer funded: 68%

- Top salary: $211,651 (again the 'salaries' include other related compensation)

US CONFERENCE OF CATHOLIC BISHOPS

Last, but by far not least, is the US Conference of Catholic Bishops (USCCB), whose finances now require further explanation. The USCCB, by the way, resettles the largest number of refugees in the US with the help of Catholic Charities located throughout America. They make no effort to single out Christians for resettlement and in fact, in 2013, as we mentioned previously, were requesting that the U.S. State Department bring more Rohingya Muslims from Burma (Myanmar) to America. [60]

Up until recently, we could access their annual reports to determine their direct income from the federal taxpayer (for their migration program); however, it appears that since RRW and others began publishing the information, we are no longer able to access those reports. To our knowledge, no Form 990 is filed. Churches are not required to file 990s, so perhaps the Bishops consider themselves a church. [Note, they actually call it their "migration" program]

Also, since federal funds go directly to myriad Catholic Charities around the country, especially to states such as Tennessee, where Catholic Charities and the federal government have complete control of who comes and where they are placed with virtually no state input (called the Wilson-Fish program), it would require very knowledgeable forensic accountants to follow the money.

Here is the information we previously obtained from the USCCB's 2012 Annual Report. [61]

---

[60] Ann Corcoran, "Muslim sets Buddhist woman on fire in Burma; ignites new wave of violence."(Includes quotes from USCCB testimony received at US State Department meeting.) *Refugee Resettlement Watch*, 29 May 2013.
http://refugeeresettlementwatch.wordpress.com/2013/05/29/muslim-sets-buddhist-woman-on-fire-in-burma-ignites-new-wave-of-violence/

[61] Ann Corcoran, "Catholic editor: Maybe it's time for Bishops to stop taking federal money," *Refugee Resettlement Watch*, 5 October 2014.

- Total revenue: $70,975,237

- Govt. grants and contracts (includes over $3 million in travel loan income): $69,534,230

- Percent taxpayer funded: 98%

- We have no idea what salaries are paid in the USCCB Washington office.

THE VOLAGS' COZY RELATIONSHIP WITH GOVERNMENT

The present Assistant Secretary of State for Population, Refugees and Migration is Anne C. Richard, who came to the State Department from a perch as a VOLAG Vice President at the International Rescue Committee (IRC). Prior to her job with the IRC (contractor/VOLAG) she was employed by the U.S. State Department.

According to her biography,[62] she also helped create the International Crisis Group. We know that George Soros played an instrumental role in its formation and still serves as a trustee.

Over at the Department of Health and Human Services (the State Department's partner in administering the refugee program) Office of Refugee Resettlement (ORR), the present director is Eskinder Negash (a former Ethiopian refugee), who left his job as Vice President of another VOLAG, the US Committee for Refugees and Immigrants (USCRI). USCRI's longtime President is Lavinia Limon who served as President Bill Clinton's Director of the ORR during the great migration of Bosnian Muslims to America, about which you will learn more shortly.

The federal government/contractor revolving door spins so fast it could make you dizzy if you aren't careful!

---

http://refugeeresettlementwatch.wordpress.com/2014/10/05/catholic-editor-maybe-its-time-for-bishops-to-stop-taking-federal-money/

[62] US State Department, Anne C. Richard, Assistant Secretary of State Population, Refugees and Migration. Term April 2, 2012 to present. http://www.state.gov/r/pa/ei/biog/188212.htm

THE ROLE OF INTERNATIONAL
ORGANIZATIONS

THE UNITED NATIONS PICKS THE MAJORITY OF OUR REFUGEES

The present United Nations High Commissioner for Refugees (UNHCR) is Antonio Guterres, the former Socialist President of Portugal and former President of the Socialist International, who began his term at the UN in 2005.

Although another refugee agency at the UN (UNRWA – the UN Relief & Works Agency) has, for more than 60 years, been responsible for only one group of refugees---the Palestinians---with donations from around the world (the US being the top donor), when the UN wants to clear out camps, other than for the Palestinians, it does.

Most recently, the UN wanted the Bhutanese camps closed on the border of Nepal, and within six years, 80,000 or so of the mostly Hindu refugees are in the US and the camps are nearly closed.

As we learned earlier in this report, the US resettles more refugees than all other nations combined.

THE POSSIBLE ROLE OF THE OIC

It is not clear to this author what role the Organization of Islamic Coopera-tion (OIC) has at the UN in choosing refugees bound for the West. Nevertheless, one can imagine some back room maneuvering and pressure on the UNHCR. We do know that the OIC works closely with Antonio Guterres on the issue of refugees in the Muslim world and most recently met in Geneva to further discuss implementa-tion of the 2012 Ashgabat Declaration.[63]

---

[63] "OIC and UNHCR discuss areas of cooperation on refugees in Muslim World," *WAM Emirates News Agency*, 22 November 2014. http://www.wam.ae/en/news/arab/1395272796618.html

One indicator of where UNHCR Guterres stands on Islam is revealed in a 2009 report about a study released by the UNHCR that concludes (stretching credulity) that sharia has had a greater historical role and a more positive effect on asylum and refugee law than any other 'faith' system in the world. [64]

Wealthy Saudi Arabia, a key player in the OIC, does not resettle refugees, not even fellow Muslims. In fact, they quickly deport any asylum seekers, especially Somalis, who get into the country. The UNHCR under Guterres leadership is virtually silent on Saudi Arabia's inhumane treatment and rejection of persecuted refugees while chastising Western countries on a daily basis for not being sufficiently "welcoming."

The UN recently labeled Sweden "Afrophobic", [65] a charge they would never dare to level at Saudi Arabia even as it deported thousands of Somalis to Mogadishu at a time when no Western countries would consider deporting even hardened criminals to that troubled city. The UNHCR selects refugees and the US State Department (with the Dept. of Homeland Security review), for the most part, accepts them.

We say "for the most part" because there are some times when the U.S. goes it alone. *We have witnessed some cases in which the UN and the U.S. government were in disagreement.*

During the George W. Bush presidency, the UNHCR and NGOs worldwide (including our nine major resettlement contractors, the VOLAGs) hammered Bush on why we weren't moving forward with taking Iraqi refugees with the refrain---we broke it, they are ours. It was rumored at the time that the Bush Department of Homeland Security was responsible for the delay due to justifiable fears that Islamic terrorists would use the program to get into the U.S. and were thus undertaking extensive screening of prospective "new Americans."

They may have done extensive screening, but some slipped through that screen. As we learned the hard way in Bowling Green, Kentucky, they missed at least these two who lied on their applications for refugee status.

Waada Alwan and Mohamad Hammadi were arrested in 2011 and ultimately convicted of providing material support to terrorists.[66]

---

[64] "UN: Islamic law is major influence on refugee law, says study," *Adnkronos International*, 23 June 2009. http://www1.adnkronos.com/AKI/English/Religion/?id=3.0.3456729797

[65] Begüm Tunakan, "UN Slams Sweden over increasing 'Afrophobia,'" *The Daily Sabah*, 17 December 2014. http://www.dailysabah.com/europe/2014/12/10/un-slams-sweden-over-increasing-afrophobia

[66] "'Dozens' of Terrorists Could Live in US as Refugees," *Nightline*, 20 November 2013. http://abcnews.go.com/Nightline/video/exclusive-dozens-terrorists-live-us-refugees-20960205

In 2009, the pair had been resettled in Senator Rand Paul's home town (a preferred resettlement site), but it was learned through the federal investigation that one of the two had left his fingerprints on an IED that exploded in Iraq killing American National Guard soldiers. As a result of the arrest, the FBI planned to re-screen 58,000 Iraqis already here. Whether that ever happened or not, we don't know.[67]

By the way, in a shocking demonstration of placing the privacy rights of refugees over the national security interests of the US, in 2003, CAIR, the ACLU, and a VOLAG (a Church World Service subcontractor) filed suit against the US government under the *Patriot Act* when the FBI was looking for information on Iraqis earlier resettled in Tennessee. The lawsuit was withdrawn, but just the fact that a resettlement contractor would attempt to block re-screening of a refugee is telling.[68]

---

[67] Ann Corcoran, "US to rescreen (maybe) many Iraqi refugees in wake of Kentucky terror plot   investigation," *Refugee Resettlement Watch* (original *Chicago Tribune* story is gone), 22 July 2009.

http://refugeeresettlementwatch.wordpress.com/2011/07/22/us-to-rescreen-maybe-many-iraqi-refugees-in-wake-of-kentucky-terror-plot-investigation/

[68] ACLU, Press Release, *ACLU Files First-Ever Challenge to USA PATRIOT Act: Tennessee Agency is a Plaintiff*, 30 July 2003. http://www.aclu-tn.org/release073003.htm

VARIOUS MUSLIM REFUGEE STREAMS INTO AMERICA

THE IRAQI REFUGEE STREAM DOMINATES

There is a useful fact sheet prepared by the USCIS which shows the Iraqi refugee numbers for seven fiscal years beginning with FY2007 when George Bush was dragging his feet (to hear the NGOs tell it) with only 1,608 Iraqis admitted. By FY2009 (when the Kentucky terrorists were admitted) the number had jumped to 18,838 and then note in FY2011 it dropped to 9,388.[69]

The Kentucky terrorists were arrested in May 2011, which is 2/3 of the way through the fiscal year, so the numbers dropped off in the final 4 months as they were scrambling behind the scenes to re-screen thousands. (Fiscal years run from October 1 to September 30 of the following year).

The total number of Iraqis admitted through refugee resettlement for years FY2007-13 was 84,902. Many thousands more came in earlier years, especially during the first Gulf War era and even during the Clinton Administration.

In FY2014, we admitted 19,769 Iraqi refugees into the U.S., the largest ethnic group admitted, bringing the total since 2007 to 104,671 spread throughout America.[70] As we mentioned previously, the U.S. State Department will say they do not track the religious affiliation of refugees admitted to the U.S., but they do! A correspondent, with access to that data, reports that *nearly 70% of Iraqis admitted in FY2014 were Muslims.*

---

[69] US Citizenship and Immigration Services, *Iraqi Refugees Processing Fact Sheet*, 6 June 2013.
http://www.uscis.gov/humanitarian/refugees-asylum/refugees/iraqi-refugee-processing-fact-sheet

[70] US State Department Refugee Processing Center, *Refugee Arrivals by Nationality,* 30 September 2014.
http://www.wrapsnet.org/Portals/1/Arrivals/Arrivals%20FY%202014/Arrivals%20by%20Nationality%20-%20Map%2810.6.2014%29.pdf

Unfortunately, in addition to the most visible Kentucky case, there are many additional cases of Iraqi refugees arrested on terrorism charges, sex crime charges, and murders.

In a little-noticed 2014 case in Arizona, an Iraqi refugee, Abdullatif Ali Al-dosary, was sentenced to five years in federal prison for attempting to set off a bomb in a social security office.[71] It is difficult to consider that this man will be walking the streets by 2020.

Rarely do we deport refugee criminals once they have completed their prison sentences.

Some egregious cases where Iraqi refugees have been charged with crimes of violence against women and others, resulting in the disruption of communities that had welcomed them, are recounted below. Now, adding insult to injury, those same welcoming communities and states are burdened by enormous costs to arrest, prosecute and imprison them.

California: In El Cajon, California (a top resettlement city for Iraqi refugees) in March 2012, an Iraqi man, upon the discovery of his wife's lifeless body, claimed he had received a note which was subsequently found to be fictional, in which the writer purportedly told the family to leave the country. The Council on American Islamic Relations (CAIR) got involved and was obviously hoping that 'Islamophobes' beat the poor woman to death. The _New York Times_ published a photo of the man weeping at the feet of his dead wife. [72]

On April 17, 2014, Kassim Al-Himidi was found guilty of brutally murdering his wife who had previously expressed interest in leaving him. [73] To our knowledge, the _New York Times_ has not corrected its erroneous reporting.

South Dakota: In Sioux Falls, South Dakota (another prime U.S. State Department resettlement city), Iraqi refugee Mohammed Alaboudi was sentenced in March 2014 to life in prison for sex trafficking women and young girls.[74]

---

[71] Shelley Ridenour, "Aldosary sentenced to five years for weapons charge," Coolidge Examiner, 26 February 2014. http://www.trivalleycentral.com/coolidge_examiner/news/aldosary-sentenced-to-five-years-for-weapons-charge/article_8860f9a0-9e76-11e3-bab6-0019bb2963f4.html

[72] Ian Lovett and Will Carless, "_Iraqi Immigrants in California Town Fear a Hate Crime in a Woman's Killing,_" New York Times, 27 March 2012. http://www.nytimes.com/2012/03/28/us/killing-of-iraqi-woman-leaves-immigrant-community-shaken.html?_r=0

[73] R. Stickney and Monica Garske "Guilty Verdict Reached in Kassim Al-Himidi Murder Trial, Screams Erupt in Courtroom," NBCSanDiego, 18 April 2014. http://www.nbcsandiego.com/news/local/Jurors-Verdict-Kassim-Al-Himidi-Shaima-Alawadi-El-Cajon-San-Diego-255551271.html

Colorado: If those two previous cases aren't bad enough, consider the rape case involving an Iraqi refugee who was in the U.S. thanks to the support of an American military man who worked with the now-convicted rapist in Iraq, helped him get in to the U.S., wrote a book about the supposedly promising young man and now must be feeling incredible guilt about what the Iraqi he befriended did to an innocent victim.

There were actually five Iraqis involved in the gang rape of a Colorado Springs woman, who nearly died from the attack. Author and investigative reporter Diana West, did some serious digging, and in January 2014, told us more than we previously knew about the main player in the brutal attack—an individual who incidentally had, prior to his arrest, appeared on the Oprah Winfrey Show to promote his heartwarming story about being welcomed to America. Here is West:

> Then there is the final defendant, whose case came to trial this month. His name is Jasim Ramadon, and he is the central character, known as "Steve-O," in a war memoir published in 2009 by 1st Sgt. Daniel Hendrex. The book's title is "A Soldier's Promise: The Heroic True Story of an American Soldier and an Iraqi Boy." Ramadon is that "Iraqi boy."[75]

Ramadon was sentenced in April 2014 to 28 years to life in prison.[76]

In addition to security and criminal concerns involving Iraqi Muslims, note that Iraqis were identified in the *Office of Refugee Resettlement's 2012 Annual Report to Congress* as the greatest consumer of social services when compared to other refugee groups. Their 2012 unemployment rate was 22.6% (the number is surely much larger, but the VOLAGs have special methods they use in reporting employment that help them show more success in that all-important measure of "self-sufficiency.") The greatest reason that a large percentage was not looking for work was "poor health or disability." 60% were enrolled in Medicaid or a special medical program for refugees.

---

[74] Steve Young, "*Iraqi refugee called monster gets life for sex trafficking*," Argus Leader, 18 March 2014. http://www.argusleader.com/article/20140318/NEWS/303180021/Iraqi-refugee-called-monster-gets-life-sex-trafficking?nclick_check=1

[75] Diana West, "*From US Helpers in Iraq to Sex Criminals in Colorado*," Townhall.com, 24 January 2014. http://townhall.com/columnists/dianawest/2014/01/24/from-us-helpers-in-iraq-to-sex-criminals-in-colorado-n1783901/page/full

[76] Jakob Rodgers, "*Iraqi sentenced in rape of Colorado Springs woman*," The Gazette, 18 April 2014. http://gazette.com/iraqi-sentenced-in-rape-of-colorado-springs-woman/article/1518482

82% availed themselves of food stamps. Nearly half were resettled in California or Michigan.[77]

THINKING BEYOND THE SOMALI AND IRAQI STREAMS

We began this section by saying there are times when the UNHCR and the U.S. government have disagreed on the resettlement of certain groups of refugees. We gave you the Iraqi example in the early George W. Bush years. But, the UNHCR was definitely enthusiastic, and still is, about the Somalis relocating here from mostly UN camps in Kenya (and now from around the world).

Somali refugees' involvement with crime and terrorist-related activity (not to mention the societal changes they advocate) in America and in the West generally should be very familiar by now to readers of this report. To chronicle them here would require many more pages and could easily serve as the basis of an entire book.

Other Muslims admitted to the US as refugees include Bosnians, Albanians, and Uzbeks, the so-called white Muslims. We don't know where the UN stood on the wholesale movement of tens of thousands of Bosnians to the U.S., but the U.S. government acted unilaterally and in its own political self-interest in two other cases involving Albanians (Kosovars) and Uzbeks.

There was also some special political reason for the Meskhetian resettlement that was ongoing in 2006 and 2007 and which had initially spurred my interest in the Refugee Admissions Program.

CLINTON'S BOSNIAN WAR

Following the breakup of Yugoslavia, President Bill Clinton entangled the U.S. in the bloody civil war between the Muslim Bosnians and the non-Muslim Serbs and Croatians. As a result, the U.S. Refugee Admissions Program admitted at least 80,000 supposedly persecuted Bosnians over a very short period of time. Initially, large numbers went to Iowa to work in the meat packing industry, as we learned from an agricultural publication, which made it clear that Clinton was using the refugee program to benefit friends in the meat processing industry in need of cheap labor (a practice that still goes on today).[78]

---

[77] Office of Refugee Resettlement, Dept. of Health and Human Services, *FY2012 Annual Report to Congress*, Undated, 110-124.
⟨https://www.acf.hhs.gov/sites/default/files/orr/fy_2012_orr_report_to_congress_final_041014.pdf⟩

[78] "Tyson Foods Victorious in IBP Bidding War," *Agribusiness Examiner N.101*, 11 January 2001.
http://www.mindfully.org/Industry/Tyson-Foods-Victorious-IBP.htm

Most recently, the folly of this large migration of Bosnian Muslims to the heartland was evidenced by the arrest of six Bosnian 'refugees' whom the U.S. had sheltered and opened our hearts and wallets to, who have now been charged with conspiring to send material support to the Islamic State (IS).[79]

One of the most outrageous actions of the Clinton era regarding 'war' refugees was the revelation in a declassified National War College report by David M. Robinson, who had a long history with the U.S. State Department and later served as acting Assistant Secretary of State for Population, Refugees and Migration. See Robinson's bio, referenced here.[80]

Incidentally, here it is important to mention that the Obama Administration is planning to resettle tens of thousands of mostly Muslim Syrian refugees from UN camps in Jordan, Lebanon, and Turkey this fiscal year of 2014-2015 and in the years to come, but surprisingly the UNHCR has been curiously quiet and has for the most part refrained from criticism of the Obama Administration foot-dragging throughout 2014, while blasting countries in the European Union for their lack of "welcome" to the Syrians.

THE KOSOVAR MUSLIMS COME TO AMERICA

Now to that stunning National War College Report ('*How Public Opinion Shaped Refugee Policy in Kosovo*').[81] Robinson relates how the Clinton Administration brought 20,000 Albanian (Kosovars) here in 1999 against the wishes of the country of Macedonia where they had been placed temporarily, the UNHCR, some human rights groups, and initially the U.S. State Department. In a case that happens all too often, the refugees were being used for media purposes, according to Robinson, to shore up public support for Clinton's continued bombing. After all, if people weren't in danger of being 'ethnically cleansed,' why were we bombing?

---

[79] "US accuses 6 immigrants of helping Islamic State group," *Associated Press, Washington Times,* 6 February 2015. http://www.washingtontimes.com/news/2015/feb/6/us-accuses-6-immigrants-of-helping-islamic-state-g/

[80] Office of the High Representative, *Biography David M. Robinson,* 1 January 2014. http://www.ohr.int/ohr-info/hrs-dhrs/default.asp?content_id=48799

[81] National Defense University, National War College, by David M. Robinson, Class of 2000, Course 5603, Seminar L *How Public Opinion Shaped Refugee Policy in Kosovo.*
http://www.google.com/url?sa=t&rct=j&q=&esrc=s&source=web&cd=1&ved=0CCAQFjAA&url=http%3A%2F%2Fwww.dtic.mil%2Fcgi-bin%2FGetTRDoc%3FAD%3DADA432218&ei=pM-KVOiePND-yQS40oCAAg&usg=AFQjCNGVym08hMfTJjW3JsY5Hrt0nutraA&sig2=nyRlIMZIQBqsf3TfzXZ1aQ&bvm=bv.81828268,d.aWw

Robinson says that the White House made the decision to begin an emergency airlift against the wishes of the pre-Guterres UNHCR and its own State Department. Vice President Al Gore, taking full advantage of the PR opportunity, actually made the public announcement at Ellis Island on April 21, 1999.[82]

Robinson says the State Department had literally only an hour's warning that the announcement was coming.

But, behind the White House decision and giving it cover, was none other than the cadre of largely Christian and Jewish VOLAGs, the federal resettlement contractors, who knew they would be paid by the head to resettle the newest Muslim group of political pawns.

Here is what Robinson says of them, of the "organizations that advocate on behalf of refugees around the world."

> Within this celestial community, ten agencies, including the IRC, form a single body called the Committee on Migration and Refugee Affairs (CMRA). The CMRA wields enormous influence over the Administration's refugee admissions policy. It lobbies the Hill effectively to increase the number of refugees admitted for permanent resettlement each year and at the same time provides overseas processing for admissions under contract to the State Department. **In fact, the federal government provides about ninety percent of its collective budget. If there is a conflict of interest, it is never mentioned.** [83] [Emphasis added]

Today there are nine members (VOLAGs) of the "celestial community" and as far as we know they don't use the CMRA moniker any longer; however, their political power has continued to grow, as fully evident in the halls of Congress.

In 2013 we made several visits to Hill staff and were told that no matter how much they agreed that the program needed reform, they would not be able to buck the lobbying force that the VOLAGs represent. Indeed many of the nine major contractors have Washington lobbying offices.

Their strong presence was made known in 2013, when they were very visible in the Senate during the debate on the so-called 'Gang of Eight' Comprehensive Immigration Reform bill that ultimately passed the Senate. The bill, if it had become law, would have given them more "clients."

---

[82] Blaine Harden, "CRISIS IN THE BALKANS: IMMIGRANTS; Kosovars Relocated to U.S. Would Be Eligible to Remain," *New York Times*, 23 April 1999.
http://www.nytimes.com/1999/04/23/world/crisis-balkans-immigrants-kosovars-relocated-us-would-be-eligible-remain.html

[83] National Defense University, National War College, by David M. Robinson, *How Public Opinion Shaped Refugee Policy in Kosovo*, 6

UZBEKS TO AMERICA?

Another case of refugees as political pawns involves the mysterious George W. Bush-era Uzbek airlift that was outside of the normal refugee resettlement process and which may or may not have had UN sanction. To help the 'moderate' Muslim government of Uzbekistan, the State Department (some say with CIA encouragement) airlifted hundreds of Uzbek agitators (were they freedom fighters or Islamic hardliners?) to the U.S. following the 2005 Andijan Uprising. From various news accounts and documents provided by a confidential source, most did not want to be here and they made that clear from the outset.

It is generally assumed by observers that the airlift of the troublemakers was a gift to Uzbekistan for the use of its airspace needed for the U.S. military to get into Afghanistan. A full explanation has never been forthcoming from the State Department or the Department of Homeland Security. We understand that from time to time the federal government must act in secrecy, but there is a larger question here of the need for honesty to American citizens about whom it is they are being forced to "welcome" into their communities.

Demonstrating that the concern observers had that the resettlement was in fact potentially dangerous to unsuspecting Americans, several Uzbek Muslim jihadis since have been arrested in the U.S. including one in Colorado in 2012. In a story about the Denver arrest, the *Denver Post* reported that 157 Uzbek "refugees" went to Colorado in 2007. [84]

And, in the following year, another Uzbek terror suspect was arrested in Idaho, where he had been resettled by the State Department. [85]

Those are just two cases that we know of. There could be more.

THE SYRIAN MUSLIMS ARE ARRIVING NOW

Again, as the Obama administration apparently is using refugee resettlement for extra-curricular foreign policy purposes, look for Syrian refugees to arrive here from Turkey as a favor to Turkish President Recep Erdoğan, perhaps in exchange for

---

[84] Bruce Finley and Felisa Cardona, "Breaking News: Indicted Aurora refugee an Uzbekistan freedom fighter or terrorist?" *Denver Post*, 31 January 2012.
http://www.denverpost.com/breakingnews/ci_19856309

[85] "Idaho man charged in Uzbekistan terrorism plot," *USA Today*, 17 May 2013.
http://www.usatoday.com/story/news/world/2013/05/17/idaho-terrorism-plot/2213123/

his government's help on the Turkish Syrian border. The State Department says that thousands of Syrian refugees are headed for the U.S. via Turkey.[86]

How do we know that most will be Sunni Muslim Syrians? We can only assume they will be, because the UNHCR is processing applications in refugee camps and we are told that few, if any, of the persecuted Christians are located in UN camps.

And so it begins…

We learned in early December 2014 that Anne C. Richard, Asst. Secretary of State for Population Refugees and Migration, traveled to a "pledging" meeting in Geneva, Switzerland and told the UNHCR that we would take 9,000 Syrians in the current fiscal year. The hang-up has been security screening---more evidence that the majority of those to be resettled in America are going to be Muslims. [87]

Nine thousand is still short of the 15,000 that the VOLAG contractor Hebrew Immigration Aid Society said they would like to see.[88]

In February 2015, as we prepared to go to print with this report, the House Homeland Security Committee headed by Chairman Michael McCaul held hearings in which the Asst. Director of the FBI, Michael Steinbach, testified that thorough security screening for Syrians would be virtually impossible because Syria had become a "failed state" and data on its citizens who have left the country are not available. This is obviously the explanation for why the US has not proceeded to process the 9,000 plus Syrians the UNHCR has identified and which the State Department has indicated are in the pipeline.[89]

---

[86] Aydin Albayrak, "US to take thousands of refugees now in Turkey," *Today's Zaman*, 12 September 2014. http://www.todayszaman.com/anasayfa_us-to-take-thousands-of-refugees-now-in-turkey_358572.html

[87] Leo Hohmann, "UN to send thousands of Muslims to America," *World Net Daily*, 12 December 2014. http://www.wnd.com/2014/12/u-n-sending-thousands-of-muslims-to-america/

[88] Melanie Nezer, "America, open your arms to Syrian refugees," New York Daily News, 28 March 2014. http://www.nydailynews.com/opinion/america-open-arms-syrian-refugees-article-1.1737822

[89] "US Lacks Intel to Vet Syrian Refugees: Officials," *Newsmax,* 11 February 2015. http://www.newsmax.com/US/Syria-conflict-US-intelligence/2015/02/11/id/624285/

IMPACT ON AMERICAN TOWNS

PREFERRED COMMUNITIES

Every state in the Nation, except Wyoming, has a refugee program. The top five resettlement states in FY2014 were Texas, California, New York, Michigan, and Florida.[90]

There are approximately 180 cities in America with refugee resettlement offices run by nearly 350 subcontractors of the nine major VOLAG/contractors.

> .... nearly 350 resettlement agency affiliates are located in more than 180 communities throughout the United States.[91]

The State Department's *Refugee Processing Center (the same office that tracks the religious affiliation of in-coming refugees)* provides a useful list of locations and contact information for their affiliates.[92]

A map of resettlement sites is available at the Office of Refugee Resettlement.[93] Why an office is located in Wyoming on this map (the only state in the nation with no official program) and none in Montana is a mystery that needs further investigation.

---

[90] US State Department Refugee Processing Center, *Refugee Arrivals by State*, 30 September 2014. http://www.wrapsnet.org/Portals/1/Arrivals/Arrivals%20FY%202014/Arrivals%20by%20State%20-%20Map%2810.6.2014%29.pdf

[91] US State Department, Media note: Launch of In-Country Refugee/Parole Program for Children in El Salvador, Guatemala, and Honduras with Parents Lawfully Present in the United States, 3 December 2014. http://www.state.gov/r/pa/prs/ps/2014/12/234655.htm

[92] US State Department Refugee Processing Center, *Affiliate Directory* (as of December 2014). http://www.wrapsnet.org/Portals/1/Affiliate%20Directory%20Posting/FY%202014%20Affiliate%20Directory/05Dec14_Public%20Affiliate%20directory.pdf

[93] US Dept. of Health and Human Services, Office of Refugee Resettlement, *FY2014 Reception and Placement (R&P) Network Affiliates Map,* 29 August 2014. http://www.acf.hhs.gov/programs/orr/resource/fy2014-reception-and-placement-rp-network-affiliates-map

Besides the 180 chosen cities, one must be on guard if one's town is within 100 miles of an affiliate's (subcontractor's) present office. When bringing family members and others of the same ethnic group to a state, the State Department generally likes to see them placed within that 100 mile radius of what they themselves call the "seed community."

The Office of Refugee Resettlement (ORR) also compiles a list of "preferred communities," which become recipients of additional federal grants. Most of the grant money, however, does not go to local governments (as one might expect, to cope with an overload in the county health department or school system), but into the coffers of the contractor or subcontractor, supposedly to deal with a given problem. It is likely that the contractor keeps a significant portion for overhead expenses for itself.

A recent list of the VOLAG/contractors which monopolize the resettlement of refugees and help determine which cities will be targeted and the grant amounts they recently received for the "preferred communities" program, is available.[94] But that list doesn't tell us which cities are "preferred." We must go to the Office of Refugee Resettlement Annual Reports to Congress to see which cities have been chosen.

As we mentioned previously, the ORR is always years behind (we have seen it as much as three years late and not a word from Congress) in producing its legally-mandated Annual Report to Congress. Here is the most recent one (2012) and its list of "preferred" cities where extra funds were being awarded. [95]

This list (below) is not the complete list of cities where refugees are placed (we know from a recent State Department news release that there are 180 cities in which refugees are resettled). The cities listed here are only those for which the VOLAG/contractor received extra funding because the numbers are large or the cases are complicated.

The ORR likes to claim that these 82 "preferred" cities are ones where the refugees have the best chance of finding work and obtaining that mythical speedy self-sufficiency designation. But it is highly likely, rather, that these are the cities with refugee overload problems or which have large numbers of especially needy refugees.

This is a compilation of "preferred" cities, prepared by combining several years of grant awards starting in FY2012 and extending to FY2015.

---

[94] US Dept. of Health and Human Services, Office of Refugee Resettlement, *Preferred Community Grants for FY 2014-2016.* http://www.acf.hhs.gov/programs/orr/programs/rph

[95] US Department of Health and Human Services, Office of Refugee Resettlement, *FY2012 Annual Report to Congress,* (undated), Preferred Communities, 47.
https://www.acf.hhs.gov/sites/default/files/orr/fy_2012_orr_report_to_congress_final_041014.pdf

- Arizona: Tucson, Phoenix

- California: San Diego, Sacramento, Modesto, Walnut Creek

- Colorado: Denver, Greeley, Ft. Collins, Loveland

- Connecticut: Derby/Bridgeport, New Haven

- Florida: Orlando, Clearwater, Palm Beach

- Georgia: Atlanta, Savannah

- Idaho: Boise, Twin Falls, Treasure Valley

- Illinois: Chicago, DuPage/Aurora, Moline

- Indiana: Indianapolis

- Iowa: Des Moines

- Kansas: Wichita

- Kentucky: Louisville, Lexington, Owensboro

- Maryland: Baltimore, Silver Spring

- Massachusetts: Springfield, Jamaica Plain, Worcester, Malden

- Michigan: Dearborn, Ann Arbor, Lansing

- Minnesota: Minneapolis, St. Cloud, St. Paul

- Missouri: Kansas City

- Nebraska: Omaha

- Nevada: Las Vegas

- New Hampshire: Manchester, Concord

- New Jersey: East Orange

- New Mexico: Albuquerque

- New York: Syracuse, Buffalo, Utica, Albany, Manchester

- North Carolina: Raleigh, New Bern, Wilmington, Durham, High Point, Charlotte, Greensboro (lucky NC!)

- Ohio: Cleveland, Columbus, Akron, Dayton

- Pennsylvania: Lancaster, Philadelphia, Pittsburgh, Erie

- Rhode Island: Providence

- Tennessee: Nashville, Knoxville, Memphis

- Texas: Fort Worth, Houston, Austin

- Virginia: Charlottesville, Hampton Roads

- Washington: Seattle, Richland, Tri-Cities

- Wisconsin: Milwaukee, Madison

POCKETS OF RESISTANCE

The Office of Refugee Resettlement (ORR), at a meeting of "stakeholders" in Lancaster, PA in June 2013, addressed the "pockets of resistance" problem that has sprung up in some cities around the country over the previous five years or so. "Pockets of resistance" was their phrase. We were present at the Lancaster confab and reported on the announcement that the ORR had hired yet another contractor, "Welcoming America."

"Welcoming America" originated in Tennessee as a direct result of the fact that Nashville had become a "pocket of resistance" and "Welcoming Tennessee" was born to counter the "resistance." Welcoming America is a product of Soros' Four Freedoms Fund, as we documented in 2013.[96]

Much of what they do is to set up other 'Welcoming' offices around the country and work to soften up communities for the arrival of more immigrants of all stripes. And, of course, they attempt to head off new "pockets of resistance" that might develop. As "Welcoming America" is a federal contractor, U.S. taxpayers help foot the bill for its propaganda campaign.

These are some of those hotspots, or "pockets of resistance," in addition to the previously-mentioned Nashville, TN, that we know of:

- Lewiston, ME

- St. Cloud, MN

- Springfield, MA

- Lynn, MA

- Amarillo, TX

- Atlanta, GA suburbs

- Manchester, NH

---

[96] Ann Corcoran, ""Pockets of resistance" to refugee resettlement have developed; ORR hires 'Welcoming America' to head off   more," *Refugee Resettlement Watch*, 15 June 2013.
http://refugeeresettlementwatch.wordpress.com/2013/06/15/eeek-pockets-of-resistance-to-refugee-resettlement-have-developed-orr-hires-welcoming-america-to-head-off-more/

And, most recently, the Democratic mayor of Athens, GA stopped resettlement (at least temporarily) *in advance*, by demanding that the State Department and its contractor, in this case the International Rescue Committee, present the city with a plan for how the resettlement would work: how many refugees, what ethnic groups, whether there was adequate subsidized housing, where they would work, how many children would the school system be required to absorb, what health issues would need to be addressed and so forth.[97]

It might be expected that this sort of information would be compiled anywhere a new (or on-going) resettlement was being proposed or already occurring. It isn't. Until only recently, the system was no more organized than throwing darts at a map of the U.S. might be!

Now, however, and for the last two years, the ORR and US State Department have held quarterly meetings to discuss "placement" locations and have compiled statistics to back up choices---for example, availability of health care/Medicaid would place a location higher on the list. The two previous reports and a discussion of this new strategy may be found by visiting the ORR's website.[98]

These quarterly placement meetings are apparently not open to the general public. We have requested information on upcoming meeting locations and received no response.

---

[97] Greg Bluestein and Jeremy Redmon, "Plan to resettle 150 refugees in Athens-Clarke County hits snag," *Atlanta Journal Constitution*, 20 August 2014. http://www.ajc.com/news/news/state-regional-govt-politics/plan-to-resettle-150-refugees-in-athens-clarke-cou/ng6Ls/

[98] US Dept. of Health and Human Services, Office of Refugee Resettlement, *Coordinated Placement*. http://www.acf.hhs.gov/programs/orr/programs/coordinated-placement

WHAT'S NEXT AND WHAT CITIZENS CAN DO

First, we need more information. Our earlier discussion of the Muslim population in the US points to the need for a thorough study by a trained demographer to pinpoint more accurately where the U.S. Muslim population is at this time

And it is imperative that a major report to educate U.S. citizens be undertaken to assess the impact being felt in select states from the increasing Muslim population and its demands for sharia compliance. My suggestion is to begin with Minnesota, Michigan, Tennessee or Maine.

As far as we know, the Refugee Admissions Program, as it is now being run, has never been challenged in a court of law and certainly not as it relates to the increasing financial impact on state and local government. We need lawyers willing to explore the obvious State's rights abuse the RAP exposes.

But, while we are getting more information and looking for lawyers, there is no time to waste. We must act.

We need to counter "Welcoming America" and give help and guidance to any local government attempting to control the influx of costly and culturally unsuitable refugees. Following the "Welcoming America" model, we need to send teams out to counter their propaganda with facts.

There are many economic reasons why pouring more impoverished immigrants/refugees into overloaded cities is wrong for America. Any "pockets of resistance" that have sprung up need help in order to fend off the federally-funded Leftwing organizers and Open Borders advocates.

Congress must begin to take its responsibility back from the administration in questioning and reviewing the Refugee Admissions Program. The law should be examined and amended or thrown out completely. But, frankly, *the only hope of moving Washington is to move people (their constituents) where they live! To that end, educational programs and knowledgeable speakers who understand the Hijra must be employed to speak to citizens' groups all across America.*

And when thinking about Congress, please always remember that this is not a Democrat vs. Republican issue: both parties have participated in and encouraged the expansion of refugee resettlement and turned a blind eye to any suggestions of oversight or scrutiny of the resettlement contractors and their financial entanglements with the federal government.

One demonstration of Republican complicity in the program is a 2014 letter to the Republican Party in which Grover Norquist and Suhail Khan, joined by other Republican Party stalwarts, ask that the party continue and expand its support for the RAP.[99] Laughably, they link the program to the Reagan Presidency with not a word about its origin in the minds and actions of Senator Ted Kennedy and President Jimmy Carter. They might be excused for this exercise if they had made a pitch to resettle Christians and other minorities being persecuted in the Middle East and Africa, but there was not one mention of that travesty.

Right now, at this moment in history, there is one important grassroots campaign that should be developed and that is to push back on the plans by the Obama Administration (and the UNHCR) to resettle those 9,000 Syrian Muslims this year and surely many more in subsequent years. In fact, this should be a major point to be made by grassroots activists for the 2016 Presidential election cycle. But, grassroots activists cannot do it alone. It requires some national leadership and organization.

SUGGESTING A MORATORIUM ON MUSLIM IMMIGRATION TO AMERICA

Echoing the words of Dutch Parliamentarian Geert Wilders, it is imperative that some respected voices begin that movement to demand a complete halt, with the goal of beginning to reverse Muslim migration to the West. In fact, radio talk show host Laura Ingram made that call, for a moratorium, on April 22, 2013[100] to great applause based on the thousands of readers who clicked on a post at *Refugee Resettlement Watch*. After all, we still have that all important right to free speech. Let's use it while we can.

Those are some things that need to be undertaken with national leadership, but on a local level, *average Americans can do the only thing that will get Washington*

---

[99] "Republican Leaders Release Statement in Support of U.S. Commitment to Refugees," Human Rights First, 10 February 2014. http://www.humanrightsfirst.org/press-release/republican-leaders-release-statement-support-us-commitment-refugees

[100] Spencer Webster, "Ingram pushes for an end to all Muslim immigration," *The Raw Story*, 22 April 2013. http://www.rawstory.com/rs/2013/04/ingraham-pushes-for-an-end-to-all-muslim-immigration/

and the national media to pay attention---we need to push back on demands made by the growing Muslim population where we live, always remembering that the Hijra is jihad!

- Speak up against the opening of more mosques in your neighborhoods; they are literally the beachheads for the expanding Muslim population as it marks its expanding territory.

- When a demand is made, such as the recent one for a special Halal food section in a Minneapolis public food bank, say no. Likewise, any effort to attempt to persuade the local government to pay for a Muslim cemetery as happened in 2010 in Garden City, KS, can be simply refused.[101]

- Publicly criticize the conversion of Catholic churches into mosques, such as the recent one in Syracuse, NY.[102]

- Write local newsletters and blogs, and letters to the editor on the subject of sharia law and its nexus with Muslim immigration. Set aside an hour or so every day to write something, maybe even a facebook page or tweet on the topic.

- Write a local website or blog in which you publish your local research. For example, find out who is resettling refugees, from where, and which local politicians are supporting it.

- Join a national grassroots group of like-minded citizens.

- Meet with your Washington representatives when they are home, or in Washington, DC and urge them to investigate the Refugee Admissions Program and other legal immigration programs with an eye to halting or at least reforming them.

- Work with your state legislature to push back against more refugee resettlement for your state and to introduce legislation such as those initiatives now underway to make female genital mutilation a state crime. See for instance the AHA Foundation.[103] (The AHA Foundation was founded by Ayaan Hirsi Ali in 2007.)

---

[101] "Muslims in SW Kansas to seek private cemetery," *Wichita Eagle*, 2 September 2010. http://www.kansas.com/news/local/article1039576.html

[102] Laura Hand, "Former Syracuse Catholic church to become Islamic mosque," CNYCentral.com, 24 March 2014. http://www.cnycentral.com/news/story.aspx?id=1022873#.VIr3X8nL0rM

[103] AHA Foundation, *Female Genital Mutilation (FGM) Statutes in the United States & United Kingdom*, May 2011.

http://theahafoundation.org/wp/wp-content/uploads/2011/05/FGMLAWS_2013011.pdf

- Join the effort to pass statewide legislation known as 'American Laws for American Courts.'[104]

- Get involved in the electoral process, question candidates publicly on the subject of Muslim immigration and sharia, and work for like-minded candidates at all levels of government.

- Speak up when your church or synagogue is involved in the Muslim migration to America. You know now for sure which "faith" groups are deeply involved and whose "charitable giving" comes from the U.S. taxpayer.

- If you have a little extra money, put it into helping groups fighting for what you care about.

Every issue you can think of, from Obamacare to the consequences of mistaken policy and wars in the Middle East, can be undone, revised, or will come to an end except this one. The quiet jihad, the Hijra (migration), combined with a steady drumbeat of demands for sharia compliance eventually in every town in America cannot be countered unless we understand the issues and get to work to implement good solutions. America has always been a nation open to immigration and depends for its continued dynamism and prosperity on remaining a beacon for those seeking the individual liberty, equality for all under rule of man-made law, and the many opportunities our Constitution affords. But those who come to these shores intent upon a "settlement process" characterized by a refusal to assimilate and adopt American principles, traditions, and values, coupled with deliberate isolation in separate enclaves where sharia dominates, must know that theirs is not an agenda that is welcome here—and it will be countered with activism, education, and every legal means available to a free people who reject life subordinated to sharia.

---

[104] See here the website for the American Public Policy Alliance, which has worked to promote American Laws for American Courts legislation: http://publicpolicyalliance.org/legislation/american-laws-for-american-courts/